A Pint-sized History of the Staffordshire Moorlands

by

Joan-Ann Grindley

Photographs by
Chris Rushton

Churnet Valley Books

Published by

CHURNET VALLEY BOOKS

43 Bath Street
Leek
Staffordshire
01538 399033

© Joan-Ann Grindley and Churnet Valley Books
1996

ISBN 1897949 25 1

Printed in Great Britain by the Ipswich Book Company, Suffolk

All rights reserved. No part of this publication may be reproduced, stored in a retrieval system or transmitted, in any form or by any means, electronic, mechanical, photocopying, recording or otherwise, without the prior permission of the author and publisher in writing.

A Pint-sized History of the Staffordshire Moorlands

PREFACE

The areas visited in this book include many villages with just one pub. Not only are these places where people can reflect on the days work but they are also meeting places and a place for buying and selling. Many a deal is still set with the shake of a hand dampened by the overflow of a hand pulled pint.

Alongside this rural life, with tales of roast hedgehog and headless men riding white horses to save the world from Armagedon, there are busy towns with as many pubs as shops. Each one of these towns has its own tales to tell, varying from market trading in Leek, to mining families in Cheadle. These towns and villages along with many more have grown slowly to form what they are today - busy and lively communities. Between the towns and villages of the Staffordshire Moorlands, there are groups of dwellings, not big enough to be called a village but nevertheless home to generations of people.

The area covered by a Moorland map abounds with myths, ghosts and legends. Many of these are well known, but there are quite a few which have until now remained the personal property of that fountain of knowledge, the public house tap room.

One of the most surprising things a visitor to any of the public houses mentioned in this book will find is, no matter what knowledge they have read about the town or village they are in, within the time it takes to order a second drink they will have heard at least one more 'Pint Sized History' to take home with them.

A Pint-sized History of the Staffordshire Moorlands

A Pint-sized History of the Staffordshire Moorlands

Share a drink with some of Joan-Ann's friends................

Chapter 1.	Albe and his friends at the Wild Duck in Alton	7
Chapter 2.	Black Bob at the Stafford Arms in Bagnall	11
Chapter 3.	Bright-eyed Billy at the White Cock in Blythe Bridge	14
Chapter 4.	Belly-ache Joe at the Red Lion in Boundary	17
Chapter 5.	Baz the rat-catcher at the Swan in Brookhouses	20
Chapter 6.	Bogey the bone man at the Black Lion in Butterton	23
Chapter 7.	Chalky, saviour of the world at the Yew Tree, Cauldon	27
Chapter 8.	Chatty Whistler at the Talbot in Cheadle	31
Chapter 9.	Charming Douggie at the Queens Arms in Cheadle	33
Chapter 10.	A cat called Marmalade at the New Broom in Checkley	37
Chapter 11.	Chucka the coalman at the Boat Inn in Cheddleton	40
Chapter 12.	Cherry-eyed Johnty at the Black Lion in Consall	44
Chapter 13.	Delicate Jim at the Holly Bush in Denford	47
Chapter 14.	Don the driver at the Draycott Arms in Draycott	50
Chapter 15.	Energetic Sall at the Plough in Endon	53
Chapter 16.	Firey Izzy at the New Inn, Flash	57
Chapter 17.	Friendly Ella at the Fox and Goose at Foxt	60
Chapter 18.	Freddy and the swimmers at the Railway, Froghall	63
Chapter 19.	Grateful George at the Cavalier in Grindon	67
Chapter 20.	Horace the house builder at the Raddle Inn in Hollington	70
Chapter 21.	Isaac the gardener at the Linden Tree in Ipstones	72
Chapter 22.	Kenny the cleaner at the Plough in Kingsley	75
Chapter 23.	Keen-eyed Biff at the Blacksmiths Arms in Kingsley Holt	79
Chapter 24.	Light nights Les at the Travellers Rest in Leekbrook	82
Chapter 25.	Lil and her husband Dobbo at the Cattle Market in Leek	85
Chapter 26.	Light-footed Ginger at the Unicorn in Leek	88
Chapter 27.	Lottie and Bert at the Cheshire Cheese in Longnor	91
Chapter 28.	Marvellous Maz at the Lazy Trout in Meerbrook	94
Chapter 29.	Osser the 'ammerworker at the Cricketers Arms in Oakamoor	97
Chapter 30.	Old Owlface at the Jervis Arms in Onecote	100
Chapter 31.	Rusty the factory worker at the Crown in Rocester	103

Chapter 32.	Ronny and his family at the Rudyard Hotel, Rudyard	106
Chapter 33.	Rose, a new friend, at the Knot Inn, Rushton	109
Chapter 34.	Sharky Sam at the Travellers Rest in Stanley	112
Chapter 35.	Suave William at the Sportsman in Stockton Brook	115
Chapter 36.	Tug the old teacher at the Cross Keys in Tean	118
Chapter 37.	Tubby the trailwalker at the Mermaid, Thorncliffe	121
Chapter 38.	Toots the storyteller at the Highwayman at Threapwood	124
Chapter 39.	White-haired Wiggy at the Greyhound in Warslow	127
Chapter 40.	Winnie the flower lover at the Red Lion in Waterfall	131
Chapter 41.	Wide-eyed Sam at the Powys Arms, Wetley Rocks	133
Chapter 42.	Blocker and his best mate at the Rose & Crown, Whitehurst	136
Chapter 43.	Wirey Wally at the Sneyds Arms in Whiston	140
Chapter 44.	Will and Walt at the Green Man, Windy Arbor	143

And a few recipes gathered along the way 146

CHAPTER 1
Albe and all his friends at the Wild Duck in Alton

Since the beginning of time geese and wild ducks have be seen flying over the area now known as Alton village. Riding the warm air currents over the castle they are a delightful sight for the city dwellers as they travel the lanes around the area looking for Paradise.

The journeys end for the visitors of today is not the Paradise hoped for by their ancestors. It is certainly not the paradise of the wild geese. What they are looking for is not a quiet stretch of calm water. No, most visitors to the area today are on their way to that place known all over the world and somewhere youngsters yearn for - Alton Towers Leisure Park. With their eyes strained for the first glimpse of the wood and metal structures, and their ears alert for the sound, not of the geese, but of machinery and people laughing.

Most visitors notice little of the village of Alton. If it was not for the thought of the rides to thrill and the sights to see within the leisure park, would people outside the area even know this tiny village, with its church which dates back to the 1200s, existed? When most people hear the word Alton, they instantly think of water flumes, carousels and corkscrew rides. Nevertheless there is another side to Alton: that of a village which has somehow managed to keep its character despite being inundated with more visitors in a season than perhaps there was living in the whole of England at the time Eyon, Bishop of Asaph consecrated St Peter's Church.

Although there are many places in which to take refreshment around Alton, perhaps one of the best known is the Wild Duck public house. This public house typifies what the village of Alton really is, not just a place to look at on the way to somewhere else, but one of the best places to stop.

Like many other villages, Alton has grown slowly over the years. The first Saxon castle was built on the hill overlooking the marshy valley before the 11th century. When this castle fell into disrepair it was not long before Bertram Verdun had built another on the same site.

By the early 1300s Alveton Lodge with its 450 acres of uncultivated land was valued at 12d, not a great deal of money even in those faraway days. Nevertheless by the time the Earl of Shrewsbury had begun to convert the Lodge into Alton Abbey in 1809, land prices were rising. By 1811 the cost of developing the grounds alone cost well over £2,000.

A Pint-sized History of the Staffordshire Moorlands

Is Alton the paradise we hope for?

Among the many sights which strangers fail to notice and even many of the locals take for granted are the Round House and Dimmingsdale Lodge, both built in the early 1800s. Spend ten minutes with the locals of the Wild Duck and memories of these and other places will be relived for a short time.

The lock-up set in the middle of the village was often the ultimate deterrent for the small children as they clung precariously to the railings outside the Post Office, balancing with an arm and leg as they swung on the narrow ledge of the wall. Mr Smith the blacksmith's words are still said to echo across the road. "If you don't get down I will have you put in the Lock Up". Yet despite the threat, few of the village children ever saw the inside of that building and just how many of the older ones actually spent time within its walls can only be guessed at. Nevertheless the threat was always there.

Memories of Dimmingsdale Lodge are softer. Where better to walk with your beloved than along the Oakamoor to Alton road, although only the brave would venture off the tree lined path. But even this romantic place had its darker side. Whether the rumour that it and the woodland were haunted by the ghost of one of the construction workers who had helped to build the lodge for the 15th Earl of Shrewsbury, was just to keep people away no one knew for sure but it was best to avoid the interior of the building and its grassy slopes as the evening shadows fell.

One of the other sights remembered well by older members of the village was the Church Army van often seen in Alton in the 1920s. Not so much a travelling church, more a mobile library and advice centre. With the help of Sister Meredith many problems were sorted out after a few rousing hymns and a few words on the evils of drink and other equally punishable sins. Black-bonneted ladies could often be seen standing at the bottom of the steps of that horse drawn van at Town Head. No matter what the problem, the Sisters in the Lichfield van would find a bible text to put it right.

But long before the the Church Army van came to Alton changes were beginning to take place. By the mid 1800s, nuns from the Carlow Convent of Mercy in Ireland had begun to teach the children of Alton, St Peter's Church had had over £900 spent on replacing the roof, and Alton Station was opened.

As the 1800s changed to the 1900s so the fortunes of Alton were changing again. So much so that when the then Earl of Shrewsbury sold his estate in Alton in 1924, the altar and the brass altar cross with ruby glass mounts which since the mid-1800s had stood in the tiny chapel within the towers, raised less than 35 shillings in the sale.

No matter how the fortunes in Alton change one thing can be certain - just as one of the vicars in Alton found - nothing is what it at first seems. In 1935 when the vicar of St Peter's Church had the old plaster on the north wall of the church stripped off, he discovered not just bare brick under the old plaster, but to his surprise and delight, a beautiful fresco depicting the Garden of Eden.

That is how it is in Alton; no matter what the visitor first calls into the area for, there is always so much more under that first layer. Therefore next time you think of a day out at that fabulous leisure park, allow just a few more hours. After a quick drink at the Wild Duck, discover some of the other sights which make Alton the Paradise of the Moorlands!

CHAPTER 2
Black Bob at the Stafford Arms in Bagnall

Like many of the smaller communities in the area, Bagnall is often missed completely on a day out in the country. Perhaps the reason is that, to the unobservant, it looks much the same as many other small villages. In fact many of the tourist maps of the Staffordshire Moorlands do not even give the village of Bagnall a mention. Nevertheless this well-loved place does exist, as any of the friendly residents will verify and like many other small villages, Bagnall can trace its pedigree back to even before the Domesday Book was completed.

All things change in time.

Maybe then a visit to a place like Bagnall is the best way to discover what village life was like long ago. Don't be fooled though into thinking Bagnall has not altered over the years, in fact this community has seen as many changes as any of the more well known villages. All communities change with the passing of time, even Moorland villages with their traces of long ago evident at every corner. A small archway where once farm carts were brought in is now just part of a row of shops or houses. A stone roadside post worn with years of having a horse's leading rein tied to it, is nothing

A Pint-sized History of the Staffordshire Moorlands

more now than a handy resting place or part of a garden wall. Why then do we look at places such as Bagnall and say nothing changes. Maybe because unlike major towns with their new roads and by-passes, almost overnight, changes in a rural community come much more slowly.

A leisurely visit on a sunny day is the best way to look for the changes in this village, but where to start? As a public house is by far the best place to start looking at any community and as any visit to Bagnall would be incomplete without calling into the Stafford Arms, what better place than this? This public house has seen many changes over the years both in appearance and behaviour. Some of the tales told by the older people when describing the goings on in and around the Stafford Arms would make even the most descriptive novelist wonder whether the facts were credible.

The locals in the bar will talk of the changes which have happened over the years inside their favourite drinking place; from a time long ago when the floorcovering was supplied by the local timber yard - sawdust on the floor was normal in the Stafford Arms in years gone by - to a time when clinically filtered beer taps and computerisation produces a clear glass of beer that is an even temperature all the year round.

Nevertheless changes came to Bagnall long before the first cloudy pint of slightly warm beer was carried from the cellar in a stone jug. Even before the ransom of £300 was paid for the release of Justice Murhall from imprisonment by Highland soldiers in the 1700s, changes were taking place in and around Bagnall. After one or two refreshing drinks at the bar, step outside; the best place to begin looking at Bagnall is on the open space in the centre of the village, but not at the delivery lorries as they pass by - only a few years have passed since these were packhorses and farm carts. Let your eyes look at the changes in the structure of Bagnall itself.

The first changes to come to this landscape took place when man discovered the long high ridge 751 feet above sea level and decided to make a settlement. This immediately changed the landscape, instead of a skyline broken only by a flight of birds, smoke from open fires began to appear and gradually primitive bracken shelters. Then came the small wooden buildings altering what was once an open space into a settlement. Not long after this came the long low brick buildings for the animals and men, each dependent on one another for their survival.

The next changes came not in the landscape but in the name of the place itself. The Anglo-Saxon people called the area between Bucknall and Endon 'Bacgaholt'. The first part of the name probably came from the personal name 'Bacga' with the word Holt being the Anglo-Saxon word for woodland. Thus the first name of the settlement probably meant "the Woodland Owned by Bacga'. As the area developed so did the name. Due to the changing nationality of the landowners and to the illiteracy of people, the name altered many times over the years. From the original Bacgaholt to Bagenholt in the late 1200s then to Bagnold, and, with a few variations on the way, to the name it is known by today.

By the 1400s the inn which stood in the centre of Bagnall was beginning to change as well, as were the village people themselves. The inn changed from little more than a tiny shelter serving rough ale to a solid building of local sandstone. The people changed from ragged peasants gathering what they could from where they could into a village community. When Bonnie Prince Charlie stopped at the inn in the 1700s, the hostelry he saw was not just a small sandstone building set in the centre of a settlement. By this time the alehouse had become a handsome staging post with stabling for horses added to the original building.

Like many other alehouses at the time, this hostelry was eager to show its allegiance to the monarchy. For this reason it was, for many years before the 19th century, known by one and all as the Kings Arms. It was still known as this when James Myatt was the licensee in the mid 1880s. Before the 19th century turned into the 20th, with the help of licensees like Samuel Stonier and Ann Keates, it became known to visitors and regulars alike, first as the Marquis of Stafford Arms and then simply the Stafford Arms.

Even that wondrous space in front of the Stafford Arms has seen some changes in its title. First the area was just known as waste ground then it was called the Bowling Green. Now the area is given the grand but slightly strange name of the Pound. Perhaps this name is one the few remnants of a farming language that has almost completely disappeared. In times gone by a pound was a place for stray animals. Or, with the authenticity of those at the public house bar, is the name a fond reminder of how much Henry Matthews sold the land for in the 1900s?

With all areas of civilization, what changes first, the area or the people? This quandary has perhaps set conversations going for many generations of drinkers at the Stafford Arms. Nevertheless whatever the area in front of the public house is called and whatever name it is given in future years, it does not really matter that much. Because they and Bagnall itself have the pedigree of age and whatever name an area is known by it is only temporary, nothing is permanent except the land itself.

CHAPTER 3
Bright-eyed Billy at the White Cock in Blythe Bridge

Of the many public houses straddling the ancient Roman road which once stretched all the way from Newcastle-under-Lyme to the fort at Rocester, the White Cock is perhaps one of the most popular. This public house stands in Uttoxeter Road midway between Blythe Bridge and Meir on land which is known to locals and visitors alike as Blythe Level. The sign beckons the passing traveller to pause awhile and take some refreshment, and a menu board outside tempts even the most discerning taste - what better way to while away some time?

Visitors to this hostelry probably think the only connection the name White Cock has with food is either with the delicious chicken dishes served now or with the fighting animals which formed a part of the working man's entertainment up to the turn of this century. Yet the name White Cock carries much deeper origins - the 'male of the fowl' from the Anglo-Saxon word 'Cocc', derived from the sound the animal makes as it struts about admiring his harem and scratching for food.

It is interesting to ponder on these words and think where they come from. Who gave us the language we speak today? Most of this language, made up of some 10,000 words, we have inherited from visitors to Ancient Britain. The first of these visitors were probably Roman legionaries moving over the country in approximately 200 AD, setting up their bases and communities. When they moved from area to area of primitive Britain, they left behind a legacy of words which we still use today. Other visitors a little later were fierce tribes from Europe. These people gave us an even richer legacy of strange words to be absorbed into the language of Britain. After the passing of time and the effect on it of the illiteracy of the peasants who had no formal schooling, the varied language which we now call English began to take shape.

The legionaries who spoke Latin left us words such as 'Coquo' which means to cook. One other group of invaders were the Danish and among the words they left us was the word 'Kokeln' which means to pamper. By the Middle Ages, both these words had joined together to become the word 'Cocagne' a word which meant an imaginary country of luxury and delight. By the 1600s textile merchants had begun to travel from the small trading towns of the north of England to sell cloth in the grand city

A Pint-sized History of the Staffordshire Moorlands

Customers are pampered at the White Cock

of London. After many weeks of travelling they were coming back to their home towns with tales of a land of plenty, of a 'Utopia' or 'Cocagne' where the streets were paved with gold'. These merchants spoke of the people they met in that marvellous place - they called them 'Cocagne' people or 'Cockneys'. That word which began so many years ago still survives today with the people born within the sound of the ancient Bow Bells in London - the true 'Cock-neys'.

Perhaps the White Cock with its subdued lighting glinting like gold on the polished brasses could have gained its name from the textile merchants as they paused at the staging post on their way back from London. As they talked to locals, did they speak of a people with strange accents and pale complexions from a life in a sunless city. The name of this public house might well have been originally 'The Pale Cockney'

Or has the name of this hostelry grown from the reputation it has for good cooking or 'Cocquo'? With staff to pamper or 'Kokeln' each visitor, thus giving the establishment an air of luxury and delight, or 'Cocagne'. Once within the oak-beamed walls, each visitor is in their own 'Utopia' or 'Cocagne'. Might the sign outside once have said 'The Pure Cocagne'?

Although these associations are open to conjecture, hopefully with the help of these few words your visit to the White Cock will be something to remember and maybe you have learned some fascinating facts about the English Language.

CHAPTER 4
Belly-ache Joe at the Red Lion in Boundary

Any public hostelry that bears the name "Red Lion" has a great tradition to carry on its shoulders. Anyone with the slightest interest in enjoying the rich social culture of Great Britain will probably have noticed that this name is by far the most popular one used by this part of our national heritage.

One of the many reasons for this, is that in ancient times, places where good food and ale were served would be frequented by the King or his courtiers. Travelling the countryside hunting in the great forests, the King would survey the land he owned, and on these long journeys the party would enjoy the hospitality of the locals who were always eager to please him. To gain favour, beersellers would declare their allegiance to the Crown by displaying a sign over the door. The rampant lion was by far the most favoured by the people and the Crown alike as it typified the image that all peasants had of the monarchy, brave and fierce.

Whether any king of long ago ever ventured as far as Boundary is not certain; nevertheless a public house with the name 'Red Lion' has given a welcome to visitors in Boundary for more years than even the oldest of its regulars can remember. Records show that a building has sold beer on this pleasant spot since the 1600s. Although, it is highly likely that some form of primitive dwelling stood here long before this, serving ale and food to the first travellers from the small villages of Forsbrook, Draycott and Cresswell on their way to the growing town of Cheadle.

Standing as it does just off the main road it is hard to imagine that people would use this pub as a staging post on the way to Cheadle. Visitors wonder if the pub has been moved back, but that is where one of the areas 'well-known' secrets lies - this small public house with its shining brasses has stood firm while the road has moved. Although it is difficult to imagine, before the 1800s this area was once part of a small community of cottages and farms, each one dependent on the well, (which stood opposite the now demolished chapel) for water for washing and cooking, and the Red Lion for a more substantial drink.

The line of the old turnpike road is barely recognisable now but there are still a few old people who are willing to tell of a time when their fathers were young and they would hear the bell ring at the Coach House past the two elm trees which would mean that a wagon with two extra horses was on its way up the steep incline. The drivers of these heavy wagons, many carrying the iron needed for the newly growing railways in the Potteries, would willingly give eager young boys a penny to run with the wagon holding tight on to any goods that might come loose.

Nevertheless there were very few boys who would venture past the Red Lion at the crossroads after dusk. The Crossroads at Boundary has always been steeped in legends. As with any crossroads it was said to be haunted by the spirits of the witches and villains who were hung for their 'crimes' from the nearest tree, the body of these poor souls often left

The road has moved, not the Red Lion

exposed for all to see. It is said that anyone who dies or is buried at a crossroads will wander for ever, their spirit confused by the joining of the roads and they will never rest. Many local tales abound today of the ghosts that can still be seen and heard on cold winters' nights at Boundary.

However one tale that is often retold when the wind whistles through the trees behind the the Red Lion and unexplained sounds are heard in the cosy bar is not of a villain who was hung at the crossroads, more of a man who found no rest even when dead.

Old Joe's death in the winter of 1860 was mysterious in itself, his lifeless body having been found in a locked room at Daisy Bank. A discharged shotgun was found reared up at the other side of the room. Suicide or murder no one knew for sure. 'Belly-ache Joe' as he was known as by everyone, had no known family and was to have a Parish funeral at Forsbrook. The six bearers and the undertaker began the short journey from Boundary to Forsbrook on foot. Unfortunately due to the combination of thin wood and heavy snow, Old Joe and the coffin parted company just past the Red Lion.

The undertaker, reluctant to go back, decided to turn the now bottomless coffin over and re-lay the body. This was done without much ceremony and with great haste by the snow-covered roadside.

After a while Joe's funeral party carried on and he was buried in the upside down coffin with no lid. No more was said until some time later when one of the coffin bearers had shared a little too much of the hospitality of the beerhouse. It was whispered that Joe would never rest until he had a proper coffin, with a top and a bottom. Perhaps it is 'Belly-ache Joe' whose shadow is often seen on dark winters' nights; maybe it is he who takes hammers, nails and timbers left out of doors by workmen while he tries to make his final resting place comfortable, or is it just absent-minded workmen looking for excuses when they forget where they have left their tools after they have called into the Red Lion for a little drop of something to warm their insides on cold winters' days? Just as no one knew how Belly-Ache died, so no one can be sure just what he is doing now.

As the years pass even Joe, whose surname no one can be sure of, will be forgotten and Callow Heath will no longer echo with his coffin repairs. Almost all the old buildings have gone now to be replaced by modern buildings along the lanes and tracks of Boundary. But of all these things that have changed hopefully one will always remain the same. The Red Lion, always serving good food and fine beers in pleasant surroundings, giving each person who calls a feeling that they are as important as any King.

CHAPTER 5
Baz the rat-catcher at the Swan in Brookhouses

There are many different styles to the actual building of a public house. Some of these landmarks have majestic entrances that seem more in keeping with the homes of the aristocracy than with the working man. Some public houses have a quaint cottage look with a name to match, while others are so ultra modern that their name has no meaning at all.

The Swan at Brookhouses near Cheadle is none of these. To the untrained eye this is just a continuation of the row of neat houses at Town End. Even the windows and chimney match. Only the sign above the door gives the game away; this is a small well-loved town pub with a good English name.

Once inside the Swan a welcome for locals and visitors alike awaits. Visitors come and go but who are the locals who use the tiny rooms? For many years now many of the local customers of the Swan have been farm owners and workers. Their homes and work places still dominate the landscape of the area around the outskirts of Cheadle. Hard working members of the community have always been welcomed at the Swan.

Unlike most hard working men, farmworkers don't just go out in the morning and work an eight hour shift. Farmworkers are always working, even if not on the land which is governed not by the factory hooter but by the seasons of the year. They are always buying and selling stock and equipment and helping out other farmers. Many a deal for equipment or time is still set over a pint of mild in the Swan. The one thing that is known for miles around is that the best place to look when extra hands are needed around the farm, is the Swan at Brookhouses.

Of all the jobs that have to be done, and there is a great variety around any farm, the one job that is looked on by many as something best to be avoided is that of rat-catcher, although in years gone by the farm rat was treated as a pet by many local children. They would sit with bread in hand waiting for the family of rats to come out and feed and it was thought of as no worse than any other predator who lives off the land. Rats have always been thought of as a big problem by farm owners. They eat the grain stored in the barns and are said to carry many diseases. With teeth as sharp as razors, rats have always been a force to be reckoned with.

Nevertheless with the help of a sturdy terrier, the local rat-catcher was an even greater force. The words "send for the rat-catcher" can not be spoken even today in the Swan without the name Hector Mosley being thought of. What a sight along the lanes of Brookhouses years ago was Hector. His black motor bike and leather helmet well known in the area. His old bike spluttering and coughing as it weaved its way past Lid Lane as if to warn the rats of his approach. Even without the telephone, bike, sidecar, Hector, and terrier could be easily called on - just by spending ten minutes at the bar of the Swan.

But how to catch a rat? That was a skill and one that Hector knew well. Many a young lad was eager to learn Hector's quite profitable trade, for not only was Hector paid well in cash but he would never have to pay for his own drink in the Swan.

Without the qualms that most young people today have, local boys of years ago would willingly offer their services to Hector. Their hope was a free drink and some trophies to show off to their friends the next time they went into the Swan. And if ever a lad deserved a drink in the Swan after his attempts at rat-catching, young Baz was the one. As a

Look out, is Baz catching rats again?

lad he worked on one of the local farms and was always eager to please everyone. Of all Baz's sayings his favourite was "I can do that." Well, one day he did, and he was never to live the experience down. Only in his later years would he retell the tale of how he once helped Hector Mosley.

When Hector arrived at the farm near Majors Barn, the evening shadows were falling on the buildings but Baz was still there, waiting for him, the sleeves of his collarless shirt rolled up and the string from his boots tied tightly round the knees of his trousers, just in case.

Slightly short of patience with the eagerness of Baz, and anticipating a pint of stout, Hector gave the boy a large ditching spade and told him to stand by the door of the barn very quietly. While Hector and his much thought of dog did their job inside the barn Baz's orders were "If any rats escape hit them with the spade!"

After a while all went quiet inside the barn. Then, suddenly out of the barn it shot, four legged and a dark shape, but Baz was there, ready. Down came the spade with an almighty crash; dust, straw and a great scream filled the air. Fortunately Baz was not as good with his improvised weapon as he might have been and all the dog suffered was a slight chunk out of his left ear and a very sore head which was nothing to the headache which was given to Baz from Hector!

It was a long time before Baz was trusted to help again and even longer before he could walk into the Swan for a jug of beer for his boss without the cry going up, "Killed any rats lately, young Baz?"

Today the sterile Pest Control Officer calls on a regular basis to most of the farms in Cheadle, and Hector and his odd-eared terrier are just a memory. Nevertheless other jobs are still to be done and there is still no better place to find a worker than at the Swan in Brookhouses.

CHAPTER 6
Bogey the bone man at the Black Lion in Butterton

No visit to the Staffordhire Moorlands is complete without a visit to the village of Butterton and a drink in the Black Lion public house. Most people today spend their weeks working and living in noisy towns with their uniform houses and offices all packed together. The only green areas these people see during the week are formally laid out lawns with trees planted in straight lines and neat flower beds.

To compensate for these formal and yet necessary living arrangements, many of these people spend their free time in the countryside. What better place than the Staffordhire Moorlands to spend some of this time, with its age old buildings, interesting villages and breathtaking views. This area north of the Potteries has to be one of the most perfect places in the world to spend free time. Until recently though the village of Butterton was missed out by all but the most serious travellers. But with cars taking people to more places than ever, it is one of a never ending supply of fascinating villages to be found.

Tucked away from the main Leek to Ashbourne Road, Butterton is easy to miss. Even those serious visitors to the Staffordshire Moorlands who travel the ages old road from Ipstones to Hartington, cars laden with cameras to capture the countryside and snacks to satisfy their hunger until a public house with a sign to tempt them in is found, have difficulty finding the village of Butterton. Even those people who look at the weather beaten flagpole signs which mark the country crossroads, take little notice of the one which, on the B5053 says Butterton, 2 miles away.

Among the few people to discover this delightful village are those explorers who, with map spead out on the floor of their homes, plan their expedition. When these explorers study the map it is quite often that at least one of the party will say, "For a change, instead of following the roads, let's follow a river today."

All the rivers which flow through the Staffordhire Moorlands are beautiful. Many say this fact is due to where they begin their lives. How can anything which begins its life on such pure unspoilt ground be anything other than beautiful? The River Manifold is thought by many to be one of the most beautiful rivers in England. This river starts it long journey high up by Flash Head and meanders through villages and countryside on its long

Hollinsclough band at Butterton Wakes

journey to the sea.

There are many brooks and streams which lead to the Manifold and as the keen walker will find out, none more interesting than the one which passes through the village of Butterton. But those travellers who follow the map and the river are not the only travellers to discover Butterton. There is another - those who through a slight miscalculation or the distraction of a restless child at Hulme End or Waterhouses accidently find themselves in the village of Butterton.

When the old locals of Butterton see these visitors in their village and listen while they talk about how tiring it is to drive cars for long distances and how hard it is to concentrate on the road, with children chattering in the back of a stuffy car, a smile comes to the villagers' faces. Before giving directions to Warslow and beyond perhaps a thought flashes through their minds. The thought and mental picture of the old men who once visited their village long ago.

These men, although not old in years, were old due to the time they spent taking the copper, which was gouged out of the ground at Ecton, along unmade roads to the smelting works at Whiston. For no matter how difficult an exciteable child is and no matter how hot a steering wheel can get, it somehow cannot compare with a horse already plagued with flies and insects, getting jumpy at the sight of a fox and its cubs or with a loaded cart losing a wheel on Grindon Moor in years gone by.

The thoughts of long ago are put to one side as instructions on how to get back on to the main roads are begun. Before they have been completed all but a very few of the visitors decide to stay a while in the village. The first thing perhaps our visitor to Butterton does is to look for somewhere to take refreshment and without a second thought they should park outside the Black Lion and walk in. When people think of a public house, they do not immediately think of sending the young children in for a drink, or for that matter taking young children inside. Within the memory of the people who use the Black Lion, a public house was not the place to take children. The bar, and lounge of any public house was until recently not the most healthy place for a child to be. It has only been since the end of the 70s that public houses have welcomed children and made provision for them. Before that time even to look inside the door would risk a few sharp words from the licensee.

Yet before the mid 1900s it was quite normal for children as young as eight or nine to call into a public house with a stone jug for a pint of beer to add some substance to a working man's midday meal. When W. Millward was one of the local licensees in the early 1800s, it was normal practice in Butterton for a few of the village workmen to send children as young as six to the local alehouse for their beer and it was well known practice for the small children to take a small drink out of the jug while taking it back to the adult!

Whether William Smith the stone mason at that time or Richard Alcock, the village blacksmith, drank strong ale can only be guessed but both these jobs were hot and tiring so it can be assumed that they might just occasionally send a little messenger along the lane towards the public house for a jug of ale.

Nevertheless with a such a strong Bible name as Moses it might be assumed that Mr Smith the Clerk of the Parish at that time would purchase and drink nothing stronger than ¼lb of loose tea carefully packaged by the village shopkeeper, John Alcock.

After the village church was completed in 1871 most of the celebrations which took place to mark the fact that the famous architect from Leek, Sugden, had designed the spire, took place in and around the public house, and involved young and old alike.

By the time Tom Bateman took over as the licensee of the Black Lion, attitudes to drink were changing. With his large family he began to change the drinking habits of the people of Butterton. Despite the fact that much of his time was spent on the smallholding he owned, with the help of his wife Ann he began to make the Black Lion a good man's drinking place. Perhaps this is when the drinking habits of the working man of not just Butterton but in many villages changed. With the working man preferring a leisurely drink after a hard day's work. This gave him time to share it with good friends. And although drinking habits continue to change as the working week gets shorter and shorter, young people of all ages are now given a warm welcome in most public houses .

The inside of this public house and its friendly locals, and the outside with its shiny windows, has surely not changed much over the years. Which is perhaps how it should be because without the low roofs, stone buildings and the stream which runs openly through the village, this community would not be the same. And why should it ever change, because this is what makes the people who visit Butterton stay for a while. A village, which, though welcoming, will always remain special and well worth taking notice of the sign posts for, no matter how small they are.

CHAPTER 7
Chalky 'saviour of the world', at the Yew Tree, Cauldon

The outside of this public house looks much the same as many others in the country, but once inside, an Aladdin's cave is to be found. Surely not even the Fairy Cave of stalactites in the adjacent limestone quarry which became a local attraction in the early 1900s can compare with interior of the Yew Tree. The tiny rooms of this house are filled to overflowing with reminders of a bygone age. From grandfather clocks marking the passing of time, with brass fingers sweeping their ornate faces, to simple farm implements scarred with years of hard work. This public house has them all.

Yet without the most important ingredient this would be just an old building filled with other people's cast offs. What brings the place to life is its people. Locals who know very little about the antiques trade, they regard an old iron wheel, not as an interesting piece of art which would look 'very nice' outside a Victorian house in London but as something which once might have been on a Straker Steam bus.

Although the treasures within the pub are a part of our heritage there is a much more important part of local history which is often overlooked. Words. Oh, what treasures lay within the memories of the older generation. Unlike antiques this part of our history does not deteriorate with time and need not wear out. In fact the treasured tales of a life which is no more, get better with the passing of time. But the generation whose minds are filled with memories of the old quarry workings at Cauldon Low are getting less; soon no one will be left. Therefore just as it is important to save our antiques, it is even more important to save our memories.

The funeral service held at St Mary and St Lawrence Church spoke well of the old gentleman, who died in a local hospital, of his long life and well loved family. What it did not mention was the name he was known by in his younger days, the eagerness of his youth and the battered horseshoe he carried everywhere. Chalky was born just a few years after Queen Victoria died. His birth place was a corner of a flagstone floor in a cottage with no running water. Although given a name by his mother, fair complexion and white blond hair gave him the name he was known by.

When the young men of England were called to fight in the Great War, Chalky, although eager, was far too young to join them. His village had only a few men to send to war and Chalky wondered how so few could save

England. As the village men were waved off he decided there and then, if England was going to be free he would have to help. Saving what little money he could from fetching and carrying buckets of water for the old ladies of the village he slowly planned his trip. After three years of hard saving he amassed the grand total of 2 shillings. His first problem was to get to the train station. Although the road to Leek was the best and quickest way there was a chance he would be seen, therefore he would be better if he went across the fields. This would take time and would require food and drink.

Bells still ring out the good news at Cauldon

After saving some bread he began to think of drink. Water, he thought, was for boys and if he was going to fight as a man he would need strong ale. Every night for a week he waited outside the Yew Tree and begged a drop of beer from the young girls collecting their fathers' jugs of ale. This he carefully collected in a stone jar and stored in the barn.

Tales from the front were getting more serious. Our men were losing the war. Chalky would have to move fast if he was to save England! The day of his departure began cold and damp with cobwebs glistening on the stone walls. As the sun began to rise in the autumn sky, he began to feel the weight of the stone jar in his haversack on his back. The limestone ridges were in front of him and behind him in the distance was his village.

After two long days walking and two even longer nights trying to sleep, Chalky was feeling weary. As the last rays of the weak sun petered out on the third day, Chalky realised his supplies were running out. Only the smallest piece of bread was left and the stone jar almost echoed with the sound of so little in so large a container. Chalky lay down to sleep; this was going to be harder than he had first thought but he had to save England. If only there were more people to help. Suddenly he heard a noise like a great creaking, he looked up, and there in the rock face, a great cave had appeared. As he began to get up he heard another sound like cattle being driven across a farmyard. Out of the cave came a great cloud of dust. As Chalky's eyes began to focus he saw horses whiter than ever he had seen before being ridden by headless men dressed in cloaks of gold, brandishing swords and shouting.

As the horses made their way over the fields, Chalky turned to look at the cave but the rock was solid again. He turned back to look at the horses but they had gone out of sight. By now Chalky thought it must be the combination of lack of food and sleep which had given him such dreams and he must go on. They would supply him with fresh food when he reached the next town. Beginning to walk again, he saw on the ground a horseshoe. It was not a dream, and those horsemen must be heading for his village. Forgetting to save England, he now had to save his village. With the horseshoe in his pocket he raced back over the fields. When he saw the square tower of the church he also heard the bell ringing. As he neared the village, the noises became clearer and he saw that a small crowd had gathered, but the sounds he heard were not of a village in distress

Eventually he was close enough to make out the words, "It's over the war has ended". The first person to hug Chalky was the blacksmith. With his great weather-worn arms, he scooped Chalky up and sat him on the anvil. "And my lad where have you been these last three days?" As Chalky told his tale to the blacksmith, he produced the horseshoe from his pocket. "You know what you have seen?" said the blacksmith "You have seen the headless horsemen who come to save the world from Armagedon, but you know they only come if called for by a brave young person who has no wicked thoughts in their heart."

While Chalky sat in the tin bath in front of the hearth that night he watched the reflection of the fire dancing on the fire irons and thought about the events of the last few days. No matter what the papers would say, he knew it was Chalky who had saved the world from Armagedon.

As Chalky grew up he moved away from the village, for although all his family worked in the quarries he could not bear the thought of gouging out the stone where the white horses lived. For many years he lived and worked in Leek. Nevertheless in his later life he moved back to the village of his birth. By this time there was no one left who remembered young Chalky and how he saved the world. Just occasionally though, and only for his special friends, would he take from his jacket pocket a small shiny horseshoe and tell the tale of how he had saved the world.

Always a good chat and a good pint at the Talbot

CHAPTER 8
Chatty Whistler at the Talbot in Cheadle

Standing on the corner of Watt Place and High Street, the Talbot in Cheadle is typical of many older public houses; just one small part of the living landscape that makes up the landmarks of England.

The view from the front door of this black and white building takes in a manor house which supplies some of the finest meals in Cheadle and St Giles Church, while the view from the living quarters takes in one of the other famous landmarks of Cheadle - Allcocks Funeral Directors.

All public houses are full of conversations; the Talbot in Cheadle is no exception. Individual people come and go, they move to other areas or join their comrades in St Giles churchyard, but conversations remain.

When any cross section of the people of Cheadle sit together in a public place and talk, great conversations take place. This is just what happens in the Talbot. Or is it? Just as farmers have different seasons for ploughing and reaping, so talking at the Talbot has its seasons.

When Autumn comes, the local football matches that have over the years become part of the folklore of Cheadle, are played over and over again in the conversations of the regulars. Each goal and save is talked about with as much insight as any media commentator on the Pathe News shown at the Palace cinema that once stood where the car park now is.

With Winter's long dark nights, negotiating the drinking fountain on the corner becomes quite difficult. Although thought as more a nuisance now to the passing driver, this monument was considered an asset to village life when it was built. Once the now unused fountain is passed, a warm glow from the fire in the bar of the Talbot is reflected though the dimpled glass on the windows. The street lights begin to cast long shadows in the High Street and the talk changes.

Locals have over the years made some very strange concoctions under the guise of homebrew. These have contained more ingredients than there have been people complaining about the lack of the heat coming from the coal on the fire. In the opinion of the locals there very few professionally brewed drinks which will ever compare with Whistler's Damson Stout!

Spring brings the great fishermen into the bar of the Talbot. There will always be a Joe with tattooed arms ever ready to stretch out describing with great clarity the best catch that had ever been. With large weather worn hands, these same men and many of their forefathers have created dressed flies to tempt fish onto the end of a fishing rod at the pool at Hales Hall for many years. Nevertheless there have been very few fish as large as the one that just missed Joe's landing net last year!

Then comes the summer and no matter how the talk begins, within a very short time the great days of Cheadle Wakes comes into the conversation. As most of the regulars of the Talbot know, the first two weeks of August are Wakes Weeks. The origin of the word 'Wakes' come from the Anglo-Saxon word for to 'keep watch'. The Wakes was originally a church festival which was held on eve of the Patron Saint's day. This was the time when people from neighbouring villages would visit a church to celebrate. Travel was much slower in these times gone by. After spending their time travelling, visitors would pitch their tents in the church grounds to enjoy the hospitality of the locals.

After the celebration at the church, the groups of visitors would try to sell goods they had brought with them to other people. Gradually the church grounds became too small for these traders and they moved to other spare ground in the village and Fair Days became an important part of village life.

By 1818 there were two annual fairs for horses and cattle in Cheadle. One of these fairs was held on Holy Thursday and the other on August 21st. As midsummer turned to high summer, just as the corn was ripening in the fields, the town of Cheadle would become alive with visitors.

On land now occupied with a busy car park, gypsies and travellers would set their multi-coloured vans. Stalls and booths would seem to appear from nowhere and the area would buzz with life. Although time blurs many of the memories of yesterday, nothing could obliterate the memory of the boxing booths where the famous Nipper Plant would stand waiting for young men to take up the challenge. Compared with today's formally regulated boxing matches, bare-fist fighting was quite barbaric. Featherweight and heavyweight did not come into it, just the ability to remain standing while the opponent went down.

There is very little left of Cheadle Wakes now, perhaps 'The Fair' coming to town with it Waltzers, Bumper Cars, and Big Wheel is the nearest thing. With modern rides at leisure parks close by, giving bigger and better thrills, what chance has Cheadle Wakes got? More than most people think; Cheadle has its people to 'keep watch', to celebrate and to talk. The people of Cheadle have always been conversationalists and where better to meet them than in the welcoming rooms of the Talbot.

A Pint-sized History of the Staffordshire Moorlands

CHAPTER 9
Charming Dougie at the Queens Arms in Cheadle

Just another town pub, this is how most people see the Queens Arms in Queens Road, Cheadle. Nevertheless, once inside this tiny pub it is obvious that it is something special. People talk about the 'family feel' the Queens Arms has always had. Licensees may come and go but the family is still there, so much so that older people still call the pub 'Fudges' in memory of one of the former licensees.

Set just off the High Street, the Queens Arms always played host to the miners who helped to give the area the local name of Klondyke. These miners who, although not young any more and who might find it slightly difficult even to climb the three steps into the Queens Arms now, still have sharp minds. Once they get talking, the conversation turns to a time when their grandfathers worked the footrails and Grotto Land in Cheadle.

After a while these conversations get so animated that a chew of black twist is needed to take the taste of the slack from the back of the throat. It is hard for people today to understand what it was like to work underground

Old Forty-niners still use the Queens

33

years ago, to envisage a time when it was not unusual for boys as young as 11 to work on the coal face. Not until the mining report of the early 1800s was it considered unfair that girls and boys as young as 6 years should work the ventilation shafts. 200 years ago, among the many other things the people of the day thought, was that the best way to purify the choking air of the underground shafts was to light small fires.

Many histories have been compiled about the mining industry, each giving basic facts and dates, however perhaps the best way to understand what it was like is to listen to those who lived at that time. This is not as hard as it may seem - many accounts were compiled of working conditions of the day. The following is just one, with a few explanations of words that have gone out of use with the passing of time and a few comments from the older members of the regulars who use the Queens Arms.

The Hammond brothers lived in lodgings in Kingsley and worked in the Woodhead Colliery in Cheadle in the early 1800s. Ralph at 19 was the elder of the two and was proud of the fact that he could read, write and went to the Weslyan Mission in Kingsley. When Ralph was spoken to by the people reporting on the working conditions of the day he said:

"I have been working since I was ten Sir. I gets nine shilling a week Sir, for pushing waggons along underground". When he was asked about his working conditions, Ralph went on to say.

"The work is not too hard Sir, and the tunnels are nearly four feet high. This is much better than some of the other pits I worked before. One pit Sir, where I worked was so low I cut me head open and was away from work for a week. Another time Sir, the chains fell on me and marked me back Sir, but that was the other pit Sir. The Woodhead pit is good."

"What about the about fire-damp Ralph?" was the next question. To this the young man replied. "Even when I use me candle to light it, it dunna harm me."

Then the other youth, John, was spoken to. He was not sure how old he was but he thought he was two years younger than his brother Ralph. The first question he was asked was "Can you read and write John?" "Not yet Sir". replied John. "Mind, the people I lodge with pays one penny a week for me books, Sir. But," said John proudly, "I was baptised last week".

Then he was asked, "What is your job lad?" John said. "Me job Sir, is to draw the 'buttie' trucks with byats. I am paid seven shillings a week for this Sir. *('Byats' were leather harness worn over the shoulders and attached to the buttie trucks so called because they butted together).*

When asked about conditions underground John said. "It is hot underground Sir, but I only have to wear me waistcoat, stockings, boots and me flat cap Sir, just as the other workers do".

John then went on to talk of the pit itself. "The passages I works on Sir, are only about fifty yards long and are at least three quarters of a yard high. I am not too sure how heavy the full waggons are Sir, but they are not too heavy that I can manage Sir". said John. Then he was asked the question. "How do you and the other workers get treated by your foreman?" John replied, "I dunna know of any lads who are beaten lately Sir. If they had been beaten Sir, the Master would have fined them only one shilling Sir".

The interviewer then asked the young men to describe their days work.

"It begins with breakfast in Kingsley, Sir." said Ralph. "Then it is only a two mile walk to the Pit before we start at 6am, Sir". "We finish at pit at 5pm, Sir", said John "Then we walk home. We do have a short time for us snapping *(dinner).* Sir we eats this underground". "We both enjoy the work Sir," said Ralph "Even though it is hard, and it is better than working with a plough on the farm".

It is hard to believe some of the statements these young men made about how good it was to work in such conditions until it is realised that the men and boys who worked in the mines lived in fear of punishment from the colliery managers if they spoke against the treatment they received. Although the reports given by the young men seem to portray Utopian working conditions, what can be discovered is that the life of a Cheadle miner, as with miners all over the country, was hard and dangerous, and in many cases, cruel.

It is not known what happened to to Ralph and John Hammond, perhaps they survived to marry and have children of their own to send down the mines, or, perhaps like William Machin who was buried in the Bethel churchyard in 1863 age just 11 years old, they died helping to keep Cheadle mines working. In the not too distant future, no one will be left who can remember where the disused shafts that led to the Cobble coal were, how many tubs of coal made a ruck and where the ropemakers worked. Nevertheless, one thing that will never be forgotten is the family feel the Queens Arms in Cheadle will always have for the old 'Forty-niners'!

A Pint-sized History of the Staffordshire Moorlands

Marmalade studies Checkley's history

CHAPTER 10
A cat called Marmalade at the New Broom in Checkley

The road from Tean to Uttoxeter seems to the passing motorist void of habitation, with very little to stop the cold north winds blowing across the open fields. In fact nothing could be further from the truth. Small farms, houses and staging posts are scattered all along the tracks and tarmac roads.

Each group of dwellings has its own feel and character. Many have lost their individuality, having succumbed to the architectural ideas of the 20th century to become one more extension of that great metropolis of suburban living. Those few that have managed to survive the passing of time have done so with a dignified grace and uncluttered charm. The village of Checkley is one of those groups of houses. Stone-block buildings, a Norman Church, age old farms and tree-lined lanes and dry stone walling has held its inhabitants firmly in place for many centuries.

As with any community, landmarks are important, marking boundaries and giving direction. In Checkley one of those landmarks is the New Broom public house, set squarely on the outskirts of the village, the sign outside calling out a welcome to all who pass by.

The view from the dining area of the New Broom is one of peace. Added to which, the hostelry is noted for miles around as the best place for good food and fine beers. Rolling fields and cattle gently grazing add the finishing touches, the view seemingly unchanged since the beginning of time. But this land where peace and solitude can now be found, these open spaces where animals now graze, where rabbits play hide and seek and birds nest, was once considered so valuable that lives were lost over the ownership of small pieces of it.

Probably the first people who thought this ground was important enough to die for were Saxon warriors. Their enemy was the land itself, a cruel land where wild animals and bitter winters lay in wait for anyone who tried to cultivate it instead of allowing it to be free. However, they gradually began to tame the land and build small thatched dwellings which they shared with their animals. A small but nevertheless important community was born. At this time wood was the most popular building material. This is why most if not all the evidence of those first villagers have disappeared.

Gradually stone block building techniques were beginning to alter the landscape, changing the groups of shelters into a village. One of the first things any community has to build of stone is a church and the people of Checkley had St Mary's and All Saints Church built. This beautiful church built to the glory of God was consecrated in 1196. Even though all the other evidence of the first settlers have gone, the church still bears many signs of times gone by.

Three time-eroded Saxon Cross shafts still stand in the churchyard commemorating the death of three Bishops. The Bishops have a permanent memorial to their lives, but local people, although just as important in a community have long been forgotten. A great many peasants died when Danish warriors came breaking down the wooden stockades and fighting the resident Saxon farmers.

It can only be left to speculation as to whether it was the invaders with as little regard for the religious belief of the natives of Checkley as Marmalade the cat has now as he surveys the world from the headstones in the churchyard, or the Saxons themselves, who, although fearing the wrath of God, feared their enemies just as much, who first found that this church was a good vantage point from which to fight the enemy from. But it only takes an amateur archaeologist a short time to see the grooves in the the buttresses outside the church. These grooves still fill with water from the heavy rain as they did when they were first created by archers of long ago who used the stones to sharpen their arrows on.

The logic of why they used the church as a fighting stand is quite easy but why the bench ends of the choir stalls of this small country church were decorated with carvings of the North America Red Indians is some what harder to solve. As with many other mysteries in Checkley it is left to the locals who gather there to explain that they were carved in the 16th century not long after Christopher Columbus had returned home to Europe.

The lives of the first villagers who lived in the small thatched cottages in Checkley was hard and were governed by what was happening on the land around their homes. The continuous fighting for ownership of land which took place all over the country affected their lives a great deal. Most of these quiet farmers were not used to fighting invaders. Though not cowards the villagers would only dare to venture beyond the comparative safety of the wooden stockades when there was a lull in the fighting.

This fighting would sometimes carry on for days if not weeks. Farms were burned and villagers were left with nothing. The peasants survived as best they could. Scavenging was considered quite normal. After a long battle many of the local people would go out in groups and gather what they could from those who fell in battle before burying the dead.

Many of the fallen warriors were buried where they fell. Their weapons, jewellery and even clothes would not be needed in the after-life but all these items would compensate the villagers for what they had lost.

The names the villagers of long ago gave to the fields which surrounded their homes are perhaps the greatest legacy they have left. Even after many centuries, Deadmans Green and Top Naked Field are just two of the places which can still be identified by local people. It is quite possible that before long even the fields which farmers of long ago would have never dreamt of ploughing up in case they distubed the final resting places of some great warrior will be used for building on.

Is nothing left to remind people what Checkley was like before? One look out of the window of the New Broom will answer that. The peace that God gave to this part of England will survive no matter what man choses to do with it.

CHAPTER 11
Chucka the coalman at the Boat Inn in Cheddleton

Water is an important thing to any community and no more so than to the village of Cheddleton. Like many villages and towns it has grown due to its proximity to a water course. Nevertheless the river which first gave this village life, like so many other natural rivers, sometimes twists and turns back on itself and does not link well with other water courses. This makes the majority of natural water courses not the best of highways for transporting people or goods on. Sometimes nature needs a helping hand which is why people like James Brindley designed a network of artificial water courses. Most of the canals which were built passed through unpopulated countryside but many like the one at Cheddleton were also cut alongside a natural water course. These water highways were built wide and straight enough to make travel easy, and they linked with one another as well as with the main towns.

Water means life for Cheddleton

Alongside these newly built canals, families and businesses began to build their small homes. Where better to build a home. Unlike the rivers these man-made water highways had solid sides which did not get washed away when the autumn rains came. Cheddleton began to grow beyond the village green and Hollow Lane.

Although Cheddleton has always been classed as one village, with its growth it now has several sections, each one having a different face. Each shines in its own way. Although the main village is only about five minutes drive from the railway station, the houses surrounding the station and the nearby Boat Inn could be a separate community.

The Boat Inn is set just far enough away from the water's edge to allow visitors to sit in the sunshine - just the place to visit after a busy day. Nothing in the world can compare with the gentle lap of water to smooth jaded nerves. This place might have been created just for one reason, a place to take stock, relax and enjoy the view. But this now quiet community once bustled with life. Many of the older people who use the rooms in the Boat Inn scoff at the idea of Cheddleton being a place to relax in. Cheddleton is to them a working community with the watercourse one of the most important parts of the economy.

Even before the canal building boom in the late 1700s, the never-ending supply of fast running water in Cheddleton was harnessed. Water mills were built as early as the 1200s. By the mid 1700s there were three mills in Cheddleton and quite a few places where fresh water drawn from the deep wells was turned into something a little stronger!

Many of the people who lived and worked in the weaver's cottages which stood in Station Road, along with those people who worked in the tanyard, had to enjoy what spare time they had the best way they could. Along with those people who worked grinding flint in the mill, as well as those who worked in the old Cheddleton Brewery, they shared the most pleasant of occupations - that of enjoying the hospitality of the local beer house with a friend after a long day's work.

Even before the railway station opened in 1849, the village of Cheddleton was busy. Standing as it does on the main Stone to Leek road, Cheddleton has always made a good place to stop and take refreshment. In the days before the main road in Cheddleton was raised, the only way to travel was by real horse power. The water trough which once stood opposite the Red Lion provided one of the best refreshment stops for the animals, as they pulled heavy carts, whereas the horses which pulled the barges carrying the goods on the canal had plenty of water. What better place for the people, who earned their living loading and unloading those barges, to relax in than pubs like the Boat Inn by the canal side?

Although most people connect Cheddleton with the water which flows through the community, to many people the village name will always be associated with the building that is situated just down the road. Surrounded by acres of neatly cultivated land, St Edward's Hospital has been part of the village's life since it was built 100 years ago. The late Victorians had a theory and that was, if they hid those poor people who due to situations beyond their control were mentally ill, then it would appear that they did not exist. The open land was just far enough away from the towns to be ideal and they decided to build an asylum with a grand facade and neat grounds. It seemed ideal, but behind those grey bricks and clock tower, the rules were far from our modern day treatment of the mentally ill.

Thanks to the enlightenment of many people the word Asylum and its association with the mentally ill has almost been obliterated from the language. People are learning to live with those who are not quite the same. In time the name St Edwards Hospital will have lost its dark shadow and become just one more face of this delightful village.

As with most other villages, Cheddleton is changing, but not as much as many of the other Moorland communities. Thanks to forward thinking people the destrucion of the rural landscape has been stopped. The tanyard, the silk weavers cottages and the brewery have all long gone. Nevertheless the railway station and its surrounding buildings as well as the canal, are all helping,to make Cheddleton a waterside village to visit and visit again.

Therefore the next time you are passing this village, stop, and look for the Boat Inn. After enjoying a drink take a short walk by the canal side and enjoy the part of the landscape which has given more than work to this community. The water which laps the side of the bank by the Boat Inn has given Cheddleton its very life.

A Pint-sized History of the Staffordshire Moorlands

Snow so changes the view from the Black Lion

CHAPTER 12
Cherry-eyed Johnty at the Black Lion in Consall

Consall valley was once called 'Little Switzerland' because of the tall trees and steeply wooded slopes. The only things missing were alpine snow and mountain goats. Perhaps this is why a few local farmers have been seen buying goats at the local livestock markets, or is it because they have found the only thing better than a pint of beer every day to keep the skin clear and aid good digestion is goat's milk. But there is no need to go to the market for snow - it comes every year for the people of Consall valley. However, unlike for holiday makers, snow is looked upon with dread by most country folk.

Most town people like the look of winter snow even if they find it slightly uncomfortable. Boots are not the most elegant way to attend a meeting and the grey masses of slush filling the pathways make their business cars dirty. To the people who live and work near the Black Lion at Consall, heavy snow will make their normally hard life almost impossible.

Farmwork is hard all the year round especially in the winter months. Long before the first snow of the winter is spoken about on the long term weather forecast, the residents of Consall are beginning to prepare. Most people born in the country have a sixth sense where weather is concerned. They can gauge the winter snowfall by the habits of the animals and birds. The way that the wildlife prepare for the winter is much more efficient than man. Country folk begin to build up a store long before winter takes hold.

Extra supplies for both man and beast are brought in from Leek and Cheadle in late October just in case the snow makes the lanes impassable. Larders are filled to overflowing with tins and jars, candles for lighting and wood for heating; food and protection for frozen hands are made ready. In this 'Little Switzerland', power from the national grid is a luxury.

Slowly the first snows of winter begin to change everything. Every tree, every blade of grass and water container stands frozen. Brown fields once alive with insects change overnight into an untouched canvas of white until the faces of weather-worn sheep are seen peeping above the snow line. As if to protect themselves from the full weight of the snow they all huddle together by the low walls and fences. All that is missing from the picture now is the large holes left by the farmer's boots, his footprints criss-crossing the fields. Here and there small bales of hay appear and lay frozen to the ground.

After just one night of heavy snow, Consall and its people become isolated, but not for long nowadays. Since it was completed the visitor centre on the high ground has become the nerve centre of operations. At least one road is cleared down to the Black Lion - and what better reward for clearing a road than a pint of best stout and a warm fire. After one more pint by the fire, frozen hands become supple again and the workers take the opportunity to look at the view from the doorway. The neatly arranged tables and chairs outside are now snow-covered mounds. The canal sides are almost indistinguishable from the water's edge and the railway track has gone completely. Across the snow covered bridge, that great mountain of steps which defy all but the hardiest of locals becomes a giant slalom ski slope. An eerie quietness that only snow can bring has covered everything in Consall Valley once more.

If you are lucky enough to visit the Black Lion on a day like this, as the glow from the fire spreads through your body, let your mind wander to a time when the main way to reach this tiny hamlet even in the summer was by the canal or the railway track.

When people think of times gone by they think of long summer days and picnics in the fields. Even the winter is not too bad down memory lane with roaring fires, skating parties and rum punch. For the rich land owning families this may have been how it was. Nevertheless most moorland families were poor. They spent what little spare time they had sleeping and preparing themselves for the next long and hard day's work. When heavy snow makes life slightly more difficult than usual it is perhaps a little easier to understand what it was like years ago.

Impassable roads, no power and frozen pipes are the nearest thing we have now to life in years gone by. Years ago even the rich had few of the luxuries we take for granted today What they did have though were servants. This gave them the luxury of warmth without effort and food without hard work. One well-known and wealthy family in the area was the Leigh's. Their family pedigree can be easily traced back to 1719 when William Leigh had Woodhead Hall in Cheadle built. The family vault is in Cheadle churchyard with a memorial plaque inside the church. This family owned and worked the Royal George Collieries. Other members of the Leigh family, Francis and Hannah had their family homes at Greenhill and Rockcliffe just outside Cheadle. With the money from the selling of that valuable commodity, coal, the Leigh family had Consall New Hall built in the early part of the 1800s. According to records, the owner of Consall Hall, John Leigh, was a coalowner, limemaster and a partner in the building of the 4 miles long Consall Forge to Weston Coyney plateway. This tram line opened in 1800 and was worked for 50 years connecting the many coal fields with the wharfs through tunnels and inclines.

Although the life of Master John and his family in Consall New Hall in the early 1800s was, by today's standards, hard with no running water and no central heating, it was much easier than that of the people who were employed by him. They had no one to fetch wood and coal in for them, no one to boil the water needed for an early morning wash, no hand made leather shoes - clogs were the footwear for workers. Nevertheless even poverty had its different levels. The poor people who worked on the land were at least able to see the valley. The mineworkers saw little of the beauty of nature. They slept in the cold and dark at night and worked in the damp and dark in the daytime.

Many of the people who lived in the valley helped to work the small mines of the Cheadle coalfields. All these mines were given official names by the mine owners but most people who worked long hours in these dark damp tunnels knew them by more familiar names, Sawney Pit, Bang-up and the Keys where all places where a day's work had to be done. Even the pathways and bridges passed by on the long walk home from Cheadle were given names. The sight of Cherry Eye Bridge and Jacobs ladder meant home was not far away.

Today both Cherry Eye Bridge and Jacobs Ladder are said to echo with the footsteps of those who used them years ago but when the winter snow comes no footprints are ever seen. Perhaps this winter when the snow comes the footprints of John Leigh or his workers will be found on one of the tow paths. Why not look, just in case and even if no clogs prints are seen, there is always the footprints of the regulars who make the trip to the Black Lion. Following them will lead to a pleasant few hours well spent.

CHAPTER 13
Delicate Jim at the Holly Bush in Denford

Once the sharp corner is turned it is hard to believe that the occasional blur of a bus on the horizon means that the traveller is only 5 minutes away from the main road to Endon.

Twisting lanes and farm buildings seem so much part of the landscape of this part of England that most people take for granted the fact that cars do not have the right of way in the countryside. Surely, just before milking time in the summer, cows have more right to be on the road than any motor car and what better way to spend the time it takes for the farmer with his trusty dog to drive the cows from one field to another, than to look at the signposts. The sign that informs the visitor Denford is not far away looks much the same as any other sign. Yet this small place is very special.

The best time to discover the joys of Denford is when the warm summer sun is mirrored in the glass-like stillness of the canal, the only shapes adding to the reflection, the cows moving about in the fields. Without the urgency of humans, cows are driven through the fields at a steady pace. The farmer who owns the beasts seems hard and without feeling as with a swish of a stick he encourages the cows to 'move on'. Nevertheless it only takes a roar of a distant engine to change this. A car driver has found the bridge and corner just a little to hard to manage and this startles the cows and the farmer is there ready to protect his livestock.

By law all cattle have a number attached to their ears, but most local farmers know each beast by a pet name. What is a suitable name for cow? Well as any well-educated person knows, all cows are named after flowers. This tradition is confirmed by the fact that very few children go through the pantomime season every year without meeting Daisy the Cow at least once. And of all these floral names, none has stood the test of time to become synonymous with rich creamy milk better than that lovely flower the carnation which first gave its name to a humble farm animal before being used for the product that has added the finishing touches to many Sunday teas! There is surely no better way to spend Sunday afternoon than a ham salad tea followed by tinned fruit and Carnation cream - unless it is a visit to the Holly Bush public house.

The Holly Bush seems to be just the end of a little row of neat canal cottages by the water's edge. The only thing new-looking is a sun-lit conservatory at the back and a large car park. After stepping inside the pub, a cool drink is ordered, from a bar that seems to have missed the 20th century out. The conservatory is one of the changes which have taken place in the many years since the pub first opened it doors.

Cows come first at Denford

No matter how good the beer, the surroundings and the company, gradually the tow path calls. The walk along the neat path is punctuated only by the songs of birds and the lowing of cows as they seem to comment on the trespassers on their land.

Nature untouched and at its best - or so you might think. The truth is in fact this little part of heaven only exists because of man. As soon as the Hazelhurst Bridge is seen the marvel of man's technology can be discovered. A bridge is just a bridge, many people think, but the Hazelhurst Bridge is no ordinary bridge, this one carries not people or even the horses which were once used to pull the long barges. This bridge carries water. The winding steps at the side of the bridge takes the visitor along the waters edge to see more of this beautiful area. Under the wonderful bridge, a tow-path meanders to interesting locks. Little bridges, many covered now with moss and grass since grazing horses have not been needed to pull the barges, make ideal spots for a picnic or just a few minutes sit.

All this helps to create a magical place which has not seen many changes since James Brindley first decided it was a good place to cut a water highway through the undulating pasture. So pleased was James with the completed work that in his later years he would often came back to admire his work.

Although it seems that the sun always shines at Denford, just occasionally the sun turns dark, the cold wind begins to blow across the open fields and the rain comes. Suddenly everything changes; the water turns grey; the echo of rain under the Hazelhurst Bridge almost drowns the songs of the birds and the tow-path becomes impassable in places. Even the cows find a large tree to shelter under. The only place that does not look unhappy is the bar of the Holly Bush. And it was on a wet day like this that James Brindley visited Denford for the last time. Sheltering under the bridge he had designed, he caught a chill and on returning home, he took to his bed and despite being attended to by one of the finest physicians of the time, he unfortunately succumbed to the chill and died not long after.

Most people will think that this was a sad end to a brilliant man's life but life has to end somewhere and what better place than a place you proudly helped to create!

CHAPTER 14
Don the driver at the Draycott Arms in Draycott

When calling into the Draycott Arms, it seems the most normal thing to do to find a table and chair and sit for a while - what better better way to unwind than to sit in a room filled with good quality furniture? Of all the things we take for granted now, perhaps furniture is the most so abused - like tables to eat a good meal at, chairs to relax in and cupboards to store in.

Unlikely as it may seem all the furniture we use today began as one piece. The first settlers had no need for furniture. They slept on a bracken bed covered with animal skins and sat on the bare earth. Gradually man discovered that sitting on logs to prepare food made life a little more comfortable. It would be impossible to say at what point man began to hollow out a tree trunk to store things in or whether in fact he took advantage of nature using the trees which had already been hollowed out by the natural process of decay, but slowly, hollowed out tree trunks began to be used for storing things in and the first piece of furniture had been created.

This happened many centuries before the area now known as Draycott was colonised. Like many other small settlements there were obvious reasons why man chose to live where this main track to the Roman Fort at Rocester joined the a tiny crossing from Cheadle to Stone. Perhaps it was as simple as this - a tired back and aching legs!

Gradually the community grew and by the 1200s St Margaret's Church was built. This tiny church perched on the edge of the village holds within its walls all of Draycott history. One of the oldest tombs in the church is that of Sir Richard Hugo Dracot dating from the 14th century. At the rear of this church is an oak chest, just an oak trunk, not very attractive and yet it has seen more history than any other piece of furniture there and is said to be one of the oldest pieces of church furniture still in its original parish church.

Church chests are used for a variety of purposes. During the reign of Pope Innocent III it was ordered that every parish church should be supplied with a strong chest in which people could deposit gifts towards the cost of raising armies for the recovery of Jerusalem and the Holy Land. Also, during troubled times, people used to entrust their valuables to the parish priest to be placed in the parish chest - even the most desperate robbers left these. King Edward I ordered all parish chests to be fitted with three locks, the three keys to be kept separately, one by the parish priest and "Two other persons of good repute".

During the reign of King Edward IV, Kings Commissioners were appointed to travel around the country making inventories of every parish church and its contents. They were also ordered to take over for the Kings use everything not considered necessary for the reformed church services. Everything was removed from the churches except one chalice and paten, the church bells, one cassock and the linen cloth for the communion table. Fearing for the safety of the treasures of St Margaret's, Anthony Draycott removed much of the altar plate and vestments which were in excess of those allowed. These items he had packed into the church chest and transported to be hidden in Paynsley Hall. When he thought it safe to do so he used them in the private chapel.

Before Paynsley Hall was captured by the Parliamentary forces in 1643, the church treasures were hidden once more in the chest. Repeated searches by Captain John Ashenhurst and his men failed to reveal the hiding place. The treasures of St Margaret's remained hidden in Paynsley Hall until the Restoration of Charles II, when Sir Richard Draycott regained the estate and restored the house.

On the death of the last male Draycott in 1698, Paynsley Hall was used as a residence for the Roman Catholic chaplains who celebrated mass there. In 1751 Lord Langdale the then owner of the Hall and the Reverend Hardwick went to live at Rookery Farm, taking with them the plate, vestments and oak chest.

At this time the community of Draycott was flourishing with the village having among its residents, shoemakers, farmers, gentlemen and a tape manufacture with eight looms. By 1818 beersellers are noted with W Rowen being the beerseller at the public house we now know as the the Draycott Arms, but up until the mid 1800s, this popular drinking place was known by one and all as the Stourton Arms.

During repairs to Rookery Farm in 1846, the chest and its contents were found in a bricked up recess and were conveyed to the Roman Catholic Priest at Cresswell. He brought the contents of the chest back into use and returned the church chest back to the Parish church of St Margaret's. By the time the chest was settled back into its rightful place, the Stourton Arms was the Draycott Arms and the number of people who lived in the community of Draycott was 520. The Lord of the Manor was Sir Edward Bart.

After the late 1800s there is no mention of any other public house in Draycott with the Royal Oak and the White Hart no more than memories passed down from father to son. As the years have passed, the community of Draycott has altered beyond all recognition with most of the small trades which went to make up a village gone. Just a few farmers are left with most of the village people looking further than Totmonslow for their work.

Nevertheless no matter how far the people of Draycott travel or what adventures they have, just like the old wooden chest in the church one day they will return. Because home is where your roots are and there are few roots which go deeper than those holding the village of Draycott together.

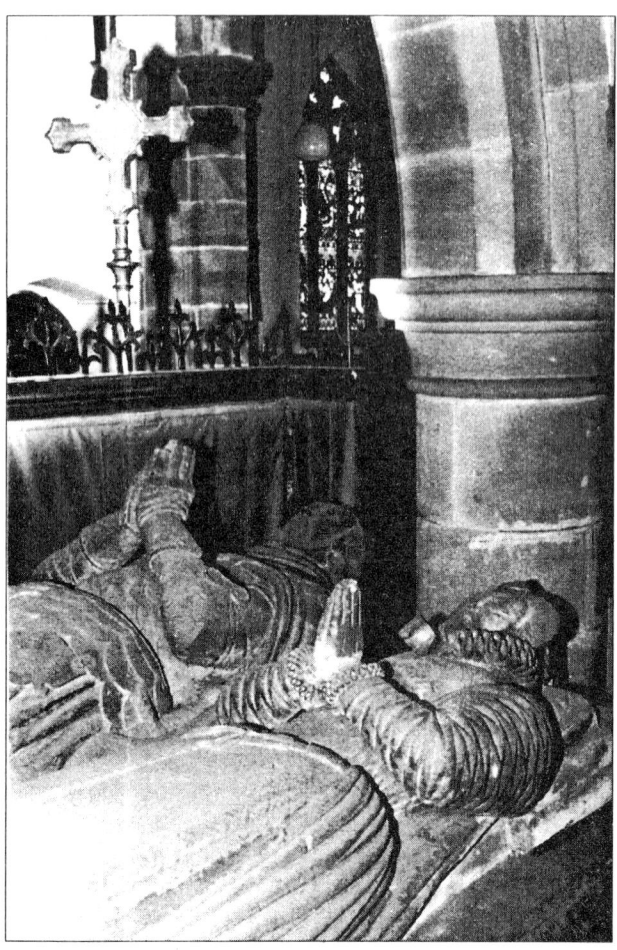

Inside the church at Draycott

CHAPTER 15
Energetic Sall at the Plough in Endon

There are few words which can describe the feeling gained when the visitor discovers the village of Endon; not the Endon seen by the traveller as he sits in one more endless traffic jam on the Hanley to Leek road, but the real Endon. The next time the line of traffic stretches from Stockon Brook to Station Road just go on a little further, pull onto the Plough car park, step inside and enjoy a drink. If you are lucky there maybe time for a bar snack or a meal. Then after spending some time unwinding, take a walk along the road behind the Plough and step back in time.

As you travel along the lane the 20th century seems, just like the roar of the traffic on the main road, to gradually fade away. By the time the ford in the centre of the village is reached, the transformation is complete. What better place to spend a Cobblers Monday than in Endon. Those people who are unfortunate to live away from Honeysuckle covered cottages may not know what day of the year people celebrate Cobblers Monday, but as the lane meanders on towards Gratton there is bound to to be an Endon man standing on the stone footbridge surveying the village and willing to help you.

A beautiful, yet until recent years, fragile community. Although fresh running water is important to every village, Endon people always had a great fear that one day a great flood would wash their village away. After a short while and two or three puffs on his rosewood pipe, the villager will begin talking about the "Flood' of 1914 or 1927 and how the tiny wooden foot bridge disappeared along with a great amount of stone walling by the roadside. If after he has paused to refill his pipe he continues to talk then he just might just tell you the date of Cobblers Monday as well as many other fascinating feast days.

The year in a village has always been governed by feast days. Although many of the feast days in Endon are connected with the lovely church set high above the village, many of the high days and holidays in Endon have their beginnings in a time long before St. Luke's Church was consecrated. The pagan origins of many of these festival days have been forgotten since Christianity came to the village. Nevertheless, with work on the land in times gone by long and hard, what better thing to look forward to than a festival day.

A Pint-sized History of the Staffordshire Moorlands

Plough Sunday, that ancient feast day in January is always a good time in Endon. Although perhaps those locals who now use the richly carpeted rooms at the Plough do not look forward to the day as much as their Grandfathers did, nevertheless some of the older regulars have fond memories of that day which always falls on the first Monday after the 6th of January. This was the day when traditionally they resumed ploughing after Christmas.

After the formal feast days of Christmas it was always good to get back to the normal running of the village. By the time February came local people would celebrate Callop Monday. Since the mid 1800s this has always been a good time to think of spring and a delightful event in Endon. By Callop Day in February, groups of locals have had meetings around crackling fires, eating warm apple scones fresh from the oven while the last remains of snow can still be seen from the windows. Although much of the planning for the Spring celebrations in Endon is undertaken by people from the village who learnt the trade of decorating a village well from their parents and grandparents, just occasionally there is a newcomer to the village who is willing to help.

One of first questions newcomers to meetings of this sort ask is nothing to do with flowers or home baked cakes. Before the formal planning of any event can take place the question is always asked 'What is Callop Monday?' After a pause one of the elders of the village will explain the meaning of the word Callop. A Callop is the old word for a thin slice of meat. As everyone knows meat is traditionally not eaten in Lent so the Monday before Shrove Tuesday is when the last slices of meat were used up and this day has always been known to villagers as Callop Monday.

After more meetings, early Spring arrives. Easter is a beautiful time in any village and no more so than Endon. If a mild winter has allowed the spring to come early, yellow, orange and sometimes white daffodils decorate St. Luke's Church as well as the gardens and hedge rows all around the village.

As the first blossom begins to turn the skyline and lanes a delicate pink, so comes Oak Apple Day. Gradually visitors begin to be seen in the village of Endon, talking about Endon Well Dressing. All the meetings the villagers had on long winters evenings to talk about the well dressing have come together and the bunting and welcome signs have gone up.

Where in the history books of today will that beautiful country event Endon Well dressing be found? In many villages this age old event grew from a time when man worshipped the freshwater which seemed to them to appear from nowhere. In many of these villages no one can say when the custom of decorating the village well with flower heads and leaves came to the village but in Endon it is quite different.

In the mid 1800s Thomas Heaton erected a well for the use of the villagers - perhaps as a way of thanking them or just as a reason to hold another feast day. Some of the local tradesmen decided to dress the well with the traditional oak leaves. Since then, the day has always been an important part of the year in Endon. As the years passed, Endon well dressing grew from a simple ceremony of blessing the well to a yearly event with Maypole dancing, May Queens processions, and a fair in Jaw Bone field.

Endon's well flows with age old traditions

Singing and merriment carry on all over that last weekend in May every year now. Nevertheless no matter how long the villagers dance it would be hard to to carry on as long as the late Will Willett who now resides in St. Luke's Church grounds. Local legend states that he holds a record for having danced for 12 days and nights. With a closer look at reference books though the truth is his dancing marathon took place in 1752 when England altered the calendar and the dates jumped from September 2nd to September 14th. Therefore, in truth, he only danced for one day! Nevertheless his name will always be remembered as someone who knew how to have a good time.

For those people nowadays who, even after their day enjoying Endon Well Dressing, still need someone to explain the exact day and meaning of that most ancient of days Cobblers Monday, perhaps if you can find any descendants of the one time village cobbler Noah Baddeley in the Plough public house they may tell you.

It is that of all the saints days which a village celebrated, no one could find one for the cobbler's trade. Therefore any time a cobbler felt like a day doing what they chose to do instead of working, the sign would go on the door 'The shop is closed this Monday due to the staff celebrating Cobblers Monday'. So if the hilly lanes of Endon call, don't worry too much, just tell any one who asks, you are marking that wonderful feast day, Cobblers Monday!

CHAPTER 16
Firey Izzy at the New Inn, Flash

Public houses have changed. Not just the visible signs of change like carpeted floors and plush decorations but those which are less noticeable. Like cars and smartly dressed people outside a building which once only saw packhorses and ruffians. Yet these things alter an area more than anything else does. The changes are so subtle that after a time people forget what it was like before. This is how it is with the tiny community of Flash or Quarnford, as it was originally called, set 1525 feet above sea level.

Some things never change like the fact that this community still looks out over the heads of three rivers, the Dove, the Manifold and the Dane. It also keeps an eye on three counties just has it has done since even before the Methodists came in 1773. The village boasts one of the oldest Methodist chapels in the area - the chapel still has the date 1784 on it - although few people now can remember it being filled to overflowing,.

One of the other buildings in the village which has seen more than a few changes is the New Inn. This drinking place now welcomes friendly walkers and travellers from all over England. The white-fronted building almost smiles at those who call in now - but it has not always been like this. Many years ago this whole area was best avoided. Robbers and villains used the cover of the rocky outcrops to lay in wait for passers by. At one time the tracks and bridges were well used by drovers taking their packhorses loaded with fine china or salt over the moorlands to Buxton and beyond.

Although the area is now on the whole free from such unwelcome characters, it is still only the brave who venture out after the sun has set near Panniers Pool. It is said that the cry of long gone peddlers can still be heard as they fight for their lives by Wolf Edge and Adders Green. Much of the area around Flash is said to be haunted by those poor souls who were unfortunate to meet up with the thieves who used the fact that the village was so close to the borders of Staffordshire, Cheshire and Derbyshire. It has only been in more recent years that the police could follow a villain across the border from one county to another. Most of the villains escaped capture by vanishing underground like the River Manifold itself does, only to appear at some spot further on. But their hiding place was not in underground gulleys but in the cellars, storerooms and outbuildings of the houses around Flash.

Just occasionally though a villain was caught. Most of the time the constabulary took the villain to stand trial in Leek or Stafford but, now and then a local form of punishment took place. Not all the village people took part in this rough justice, just a few, and according to the unwritten history books of Flash, it did not take place too often and then under the cover of darkness for fear that the village elders might find out. A few villagers acted as judge and jury and on windswept nights when the moon was hidden by heavy clouds, a rope was called for and someone had to meet his maker.

In the early 1700s in the large towns and cities a hangman was a respected member of the community, for as he often said, 'It was never the hangman who hung the villain, it was the Law'. The hangman, who would visit when needed, kept his hemp rope carefully oiled in a wicker basket - it would not do if he bungled his job; the correct form of death from a hangman's rope was a broken neck. This is where a hangman took pride in his job. But not so when it was village locals doing the job. More often than not after the villain had been given a short time to repent his sins, a makeshift gallows was picked, a sturdy tree at the crossing of two tracks was picked out and the deed would be done. After official hangings, sometimes, when the hangman had retrieved his rope, the body would be taken to a high place and suspended on a gibbet, a tree where it was left to rot. In the villages, the body was left where it hung as a warning to other villains.

Nothing is left of that awful part of Moorland history; not even the oldest of the inhabitants of Flash think of the village as anything other than a quiet spot on the landscape now. As they sit in the cosy rooms, few of the conversations go back further than the day decimalisation came to Flash in 1971. Just like the counterfeit coins which were one of the main trades in the village in years gone by, this new coinage glinted just a bit too much. With its uniform shape and names it had no soul and although very practical these new coins were far too small and uninteresting in comparison with large brown pennies and farthings, silver tanners and bobs, large half crowns, and for the rich, crowns. No matter how decorative the new coins are, where is the fun in collecting coins which all look the same. One of the favourite games played in years gone by was sorting the coins out. On a good evening in the New Inn around a table the dates on the coins could range from very worn Victoria Bun Pennies to shiny threepenny pieces with Queen Elizabeth II face on them. Ask any of the older regulars and they will tell you that this new money, as many still call it, does not smell right. The coppery smell of old money was something even the best forfeiter could not imitate.

Subtly but surely, though, this will change. When most of the locals in a few years have no coins in their pockets only paper or even plastic money, they will be heard to say "It was not like this in my day; there was nothing wrong with proper money like 50p pieces and one pound coins!"

It has not always been peaceful around Flash

CHAPTER 17
Friendly Ella at the Fox and Goose at Foxt

What better way is there to spend a Summer's evening than a drive from Froghall to Leek? But next time instead of taking the main road use the smaller lanes decorated with their wild flowers and visit some of the wonderful places which make up the delightful map of the Moorlands. The village lanes welcome visitors with their white clock heads of windswept dandelions and tall golden rods blowing in the evening breeze and the place names give the traveller a glimpse of village life of long ago.

The tiny village of Foxt is one of these places. As well as clumps of wildflowers scattered between the cottages, there are places with names like Shirley Brook, Cote Field and Fernylee, speaking of a time long when man deeply loved the land around the place he lived in, with little thought for anything beyond the village of his birth.

As the drive takes the visitor towards the Fox and Goose public house, the mind works on these words and wonders what they meant to those village people of long ago. Shirley Brook, that delightful area which

Will the little people come back to Foxt one day?

forms a natural boundary between Foxt and Whiston is quite easy - the Old English words describe what a place was like - 'the area which shines on the lea side of the wood by the brook', became Shirley Brook.

Many of the other areas around the village are just as easy to identify. Some places within the boundary of Foxt though are are not quite what they seem at first. Wall Field and Stocking Meadow owe more to the Old English words 'Waella' meaning a well and the Anglo Saxon word 'Stoc', a stick or stump of a tree, than a dividing barrier of stones and an item of clothes. The meaning of the village name itself seems at first sight easy to work out. Foxt just means Fox from the Anglo Saxon word Feax meaning a hairy animal, with the T added as an after thought. Nevertheless records dated as early as 1179 give the name of the area as 'Foxwiss' which translated into the language of today becomes not the animal itself but the lair of the animal with the Old English word Foxiate another name the area was known by, which translates to the mouth or gate of the fox lair. After a few variants on the way, by the mid 1500s the area had become known by the name we use today.

Few people can travel through the village of Foxt and pass the Fox and Goose without stopping. Many people think it was given its lovely name long ago to describe the two animals which seem so much a part of the countryside that people sometimes forget just how fierce a full grown goose is and what a threat to the farmer the fox can be. Yet the name of this public house is modern compared with some of the landmarks of Foxt. No trace of a public house called the Fox and Goose can be found in the report given when two local gentlemen walked the boundary in the late 1700s - what William Goodwin and William Wheildon saw opposite the packhorse stables was the Hollybush Inn.

Talk to some of the locals and they will give you different reasons why this public house was given the name Fox and Goose. One reason given is that it was because so few weeks went by, years ago, without tales being taken into the house of how the foxes were getting into Gate Farm. Of all the poultry kept on the farm only the farm goose stood any chance against the fox, with its outstretched wings, large beak and a cackle which can be heard at Whirley Low and Lane Ends. Even the wildest of foxes who live in Blackbank Wood feared a full sized goose!

Another reason given, and a much more romantic one, has nothing to do with the foxes who still run free in the wooded areas between Foxt and Clough Head Brook. It is that the name is a variant of the words Fairy Folk and Goose. Most tales and legends told in the bar of the Fox and Goose are told by the older gentlemen of the village but some tales are given a softer angle - there is no better story teller than a lady and Foxt is noted for them.

Only a few years have passed since Ella last sat in the bar of the Fox and Goose at lunch time. Once she had a port and lemon in her hand she would willingly talk of her childhood in Foxt. Her playgrounds were the site of the old Manor House, Holloway, Milking Lane and the Malthouse behind the Fox and Goose. As the slice of lemon moved slowly down the glass, Ella would tell of how she knew where, by the pond under some of fallen trees, there once lived the little people.

To begin a conversation, and more often than not, a drink, Ella would say, "It has been quite a few years since the little folk of Foxt have been seen." This would guarantee the question, "What little folk?" With a smile as broad as Spout Gutter, Ella would begin her tale. Ella was one of the few grown people who would ever admit to having ever seen the village fairies. Or even admit that the tall Foxgloves which once grew behind the long gone Primitive Methodist Chapel, and often found by the the side of the blacksmiths shop, were dropped by the fairies as they moved on to their summer quarters by the pond.

According to Ella, the tiny folk once inhabited the village alongside the townspeople. Tiny souls with clothes and names which would give them cover any time they choose. Names such as Wood Anemone, Bluebell and Violet were all well-used names of the fairy folk according to Ella. Although tiny, these folk were not frightened of the farm geese. In fact many a fairy shared the downy feathers on the back of a goose with the goslings when travelling from one part of the village to another. And this is how the Hollybush changed its name when these tiny folk and a large white goose were seen together.

When asked where the fairy folk are now, Ella would smile as she recalled the the day of King George's Silver Jubilee in June 1935. After the thanksgiving service in the church and tea in St Mark's school, the celebrations meandered around the village till late into the evening. The noise of dancing and singing so disturbed the little folk that they gathered up their belongings and borrowed one of the geese from Bolton Farm and moved on to a new home past Fiddlers Plot.

Ella is now gone but her memory will live for as long as people pass the tale on about the day the little folk rode out of Foxt to their new home on the back of a goose.

CHAPTER 18
Freddy and the swimmers at the Railway in Froghall

Just the same as any other railway, the Railway public house at Froghall carries people. But on this railway people are not looking at timetables and watches and getting agitated if they wait too long. No, once inside, people want to stay for as long as possible! Comfortable seats around rooms filled with interesting people holds no likeness to any cold intercity train.

People might imagine that the talk in this public house would be connected with that great invention which the genius George Stephenson gave to the world in the 1829. But only occasionally do the regulars talk of how Stephenson's Rocket was to change the speed at which people where to move from one part of the country to an other. As was said at the time "From the speed of a carthorse to that of a racehorse". Even that other railway, which at one time was essential for the extraction of minerals out of the ground, is only occasionally talked about now. Yet without those minerals gouged out of the ground there would have been no Railway public house at Froghall.

Most of the time the main topic of conversation in the Railway is people. Not the great people who revolutionise lives or even the politicians in London who make the decisions which change the way the people in Froghall live. Even politicians like William Huskisson are little remembered as they sip their drinks. This man, it was said, was the first Railway casualty when in 1830 he was knocked down and killed by the train the 'Fury' as it made its first journey on the Liverpool to Manchester track. No, the locals who use the Railway talk about people who lived and worked and played by the canal.

At one time the best public house historians in the Railway could remember what it was like to live and work in a time before the motor car brought the workers into Boltons works and how people managed in Froghall when the General Strike loomed. Nor, due to the passing of time, are there many people who can talk of how things were before a day which was to change the course of history - a day in December 1936. The few people in Froghall who had a radio listened with disbelief as the uncrowned King Edward VIII declared his love for Mrs Simpson in preference to the Crown.

Just as the country had settled down again and King George VI

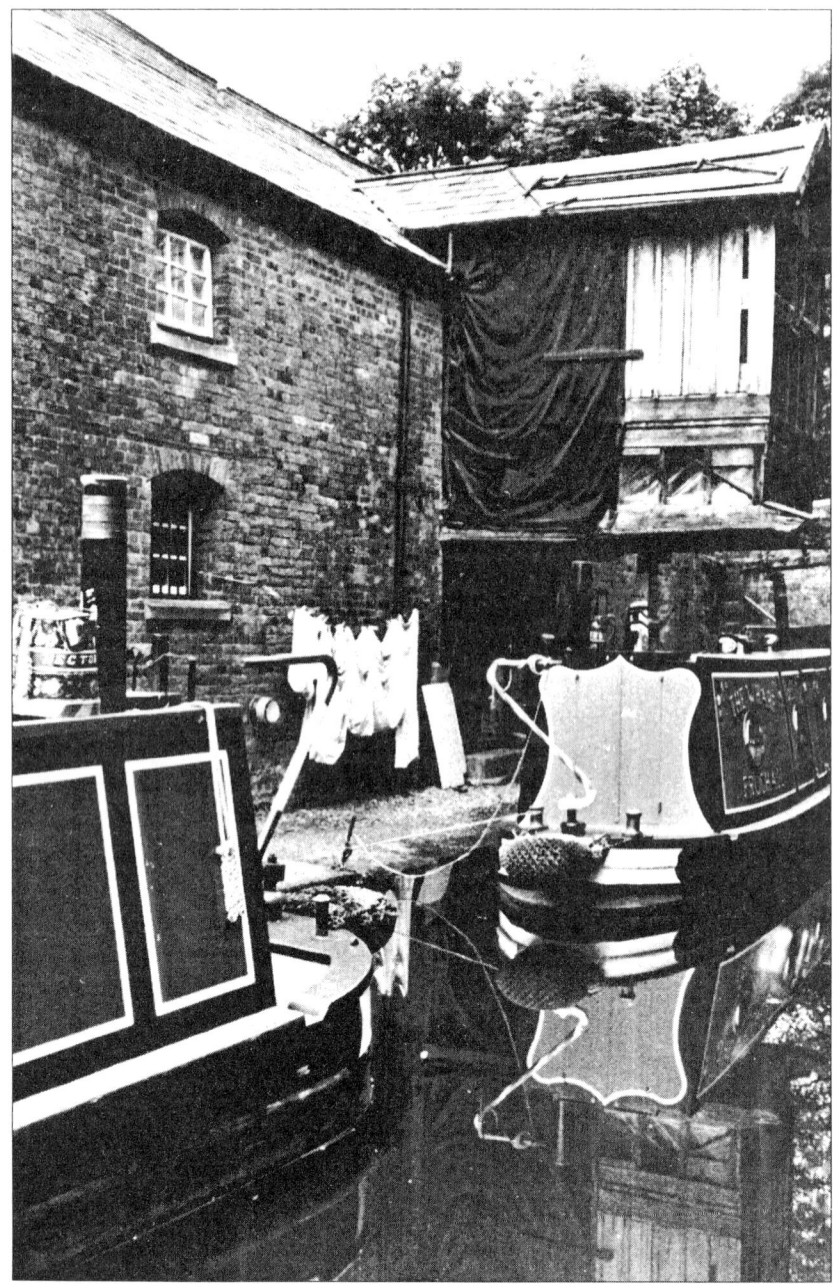

A Pint-sized History of the Staffordshire Moorlands

You don't see many knitted swimsuits at Froghall nowadays

A Pint-sized History of the Staffordshire Moorlands

came to the throne, so came the War. To many villagers, the events in London and Germany seemed far off making only a small difference to the way people lived. The young boys and girls of Froghall would, instead of playing cowboys and indians around the canal side, take the parts of dashing young fighter commanders with make-shift binoculars, searching the skies to look for the first sight of a Messerschmidt over the wharf.

But as the war progressed changes were to come to the community of Froghall. A new style of dress was seen in the Railway. Young men on leave from the war would, after arriving at Froghall Station in battledress, call into the public house before going home to spend just a short time with their family before returning overseas again. Old friends to see and new friends to make and all in such a short time.

Young people from the worst hit areas of the country such as London were sent to find accommodation in the safety of the countryside. These children made great playmates for the Froghall children even if they were slightly unaccustomed to the simplicity of country life. One of the differences between city children and the locals was that the city children had little need to learn to swim whereas most Froghall children learnt from an early age what a great deal of fun can be had in a quiet corner of a canal.

The three boys who lived by the station loved nothing better than an afternoon swim in the Caldon Canal. Few of the children of Froghall had swimming costumes - what was the point of a swimming costume when short trousers dried quickly on the way home. Names are somehow unimportant when you are young and the girl with the cockney accent didn't need a name but what she did need, if she was ever going to help to capture the Germans who, according to the boys, lived in the wooded area on the other side of the canal, was a boat to sail and a swimming costume.

After a few days away from the canal side den which the boys had created from chicken wire, wood and hedge, the girl came back and disrobed to reveal a grey and bottle green striped knitted swimming costume. The girl told the boys in her strange accent that the lady she lodged with had been kind enough to knit it for her. The boys tried not to laugh at this gangling girl with a large white ribbon in hair and the strangest garment they had ever seen.

Now what about the boat? This the girl said was easy. On the shed door outside one of the houses she passed on her way to the den was the best boat she had ever seen. This the boys said they must see, so they went to look and sure enough, by the outhouse door of one of the houses, stood a small rowing boat. Well, the group thought, it was wartime and the boys had heard of the government commandeering things, so why not a boat.

As the three boys in their shorts jumped into the boat the girls job was to launch the craft and then jump in. This should have been a smooth operation if the bank side had not been slippy. The girl missed her foot and in the canal she went. First one boy then another shouted, 'swim', as the white ribbon bobbed up and down into the dark water. After a while the girl screamed "I never learned!!"

Leaning over the side of the craft one of the boys made a grab for the back of the swimming costume and pulled and pulled, but the girl still stayed where she was while the swimming costume grew and grew. The other two boys climbed out of the boat and one held the girl around the waist while the other dragged her by the hand to the bank side.

Eventually the girl, the three boys and the boat were on dry land, but what a sorry sight they made. The poor girl was worst off, most of the bottle green colour had come out of the swimming costume and turned her legs arms and chest a stripey green colour. The large white hair ribbon hung limply down over her face and the weight of the water had made her hand-knitted swimming costume grow enormously. The once neat, if gaudy, outfit had grown so much, what was once the waist was now somewhere below her knees!

Gathering her dress she stood behind a tree and tried to get the elongated swimsuit off and her dress back on again, shouting that, "she did not care if the Germans took over the whole of Froghall; she would never, never get into a boat again". The boys dragged the boat back to the yard and hung it back on the outhouse door before the owner returned from work.

Even before the war ended the girl disappeared from the canal sides of Froghall with the boys finding that was to be the last summer looking for spies at Froghall. The next time they were to go sailing was when they emigrated to Australia. It was to be a long time before they paid a visit to the Railway again, but after a pint of best bitter they walked once more to the waterside to look for any traces of yesteryear; but nothing was left of that last summer of childhood. Only the echos of a cockney voice and a smile when any one mentioned bottle green swimming costumes!

CHAPTER 19
Grateful George at the Cavalier in Grindon

If any Moorland village suits its name it has to be the village of Grindon. With grit-like soil only the hardiest of plants grow; not for Grindon the delicate fuchsias and lilies of town gardens, the best growing plants in this Moorland village are gorses and heather. With an even grittier resilience, the people of this village created a community against all odds. Set high on the windswept hills overlooking the River Hamps, many visitors pass through the village without giving it a second look but the next time you are out travelling on the Leek to Ashbourne road and the signs direct you to Grindon, spend some time looking around this charming little village.

Once in the village, it does not take the visitor long to find the public house. Until recently it was called the Green Man but although, like many public houses, its name has changed and despite its modern facilities, it still manages to retain the charm bestowed on it over the years.

Although it is not the easiest thing to do first before calling into the Cavalier, take a walk around the delightful village, firstly to see the beautiful church surrounded by a solid greystone wall and wooden gates. This church was built in 1831 to replace a much earlier one. Decorated with gargoyles whose faces seem to laugh at passers by and with delicate angels who seem to carry the weight of the chancel roof as though there were no more pleasurable thing to do for eternity, it all makes a moving sight.

Most visitors to Grindon will agree that there is no sight more breathtaking than the spire of this church. The best time to look at it is when it is silhouetted against a red streaked sky on a warm summer's evening. Even a great artist would struggle to capture the beauty of the sight as the sky around Grindon changes from the bright blue and white of a summer's day, through yellow, pink, orange and then blood red before the first evening stars appear in the sky around the church. The bark of the tall sycamore trees, and the wings of the starlings in them, surround the church and somehow reflect back all those colours of the sky around Grindon.

Even on the clearest of days the spire of the village church, which reaches at its highest point 1050 feet above see level, seems somehow to pierce the clouds as they race across the sky. Visitors have no choice but to look skyward when they begin the slight incline which leads to the church gate. Once within those gates the first thing people do as they walk along the stone-slabbed path, is to look at the gravestones in the church grounds, thinking about the lives of the people resting there. With the passing of time softening even the most tragic of family deaths recorded on the headstones, looking at old gravestones can be a pleasant way to spend an hour.

Looking skyward at Grindon

A Pint-sized History of the Staffordshire Moorlands

There is one memorial within the church, though, which is quite recent. It bears the date 1947, which causes visitors to pause a while and think. Most visitors over the age of 50 can remember something of that year, but why in this tiny remote village is there a memorial to eight crew members of a Halifax aeroplane? The best way to find out is to go out of the church and walk to the Cavalier. Once comfortably seated around a table with a drink, one of the older members of this village will only be to glad to tell their version of the day the winter skyline of Grindon changed in a split second from a pure white blanket of snow to a great ball of flame-red fire.

The winter of 1947 will be remembered by most people as the hardest in living memory with snow covering everything. Most city people have a tale to tell about that winter with the height of snow getting higher as the years pass! For the people of Grindon though, that winter brought more than just snow burying the walls, gates and even the outhouses of the village. The winter of 1947 will always be remembered as the time when people outside the village forgot just how village people can survive without outside help. Because of the deep snowdrifts, no supplies were getting into many of the remotest villages. After a food drop at Longnor, a Halifax plane from the R.A.F. flew over Grindon Moor. Within seconds it was too late, the wing of the plane had touched something, perhaps the whiteness of the snow had caused a slight misjudgment by the pilot of the distance between the plane and the ground. As the villagers watched in disbelief, a ball of flame filled the sky and the air was thick with the acrid smell of burning rubber. The crash killed all those on board. Although deep sorrow was felt in the village, there was, and still is, a slight tinge of anger at the waste as the villagers to this day insist that they could have survived with the stockpiles of food they had. Nevertheless they will never forget that day in February 1947 when eight brave young men gave their lives for Grindon.

After the older people of the village have told their tale, the only thing left to do is to go back to the church and look again at that memorial which says 'In Grateful Remembrance' and do as many local people still do; read each name slowly and then thank each man personally for what they tried to do that day. For although most of the visitors to Grindon will say that the day the R.A.F. lost eight men has nothing to do with them, the fact that they gave their lives should have an effect on them, because it should give each person who visits Grindon a sense of pride to think that even without waiting, some people are prepared to risk everything for the benefit of others.

CHAPTER 20
Horace the house builder at the Raddle Inn in Hollington

Many a weary traveller has paused outside the Raddle Inn in Hollington but not for long. In the time it takes to look up at the sign over the door, the traveller has walked inside. The friendly atmosphere of this public house almost comes out and guides the visitor in. What makes this little part of the Staffordshire Moorlands so special? Even the name of the public house is special. Not for the people of Hollington a name with no meaning, a name given to their drinking place just for convenience.

No, the word Raddle comes from a language which with the passing of time is fast disappearing. In times gone by a country raddle was a small stream which ran over stones. This word grew from the old German word 'Radeln' which translated becomes to sift or to riddle. A lovely meaning for a lovely country pub; it gives the sign outside the door a new dimension.

One of the reasons visitors call into this public house is that they are on their way to the remains of the beautiful Croxden Abbey which stands close by. Founded in the late 1100s by the Cistercian order of monks, the Abbey is the final resting place of the crusader who ordered the building to take place - Bertram de Verdum is said to be buried behind the High Altar at the Abbey. Among the many things this man is remembered for, perhaps the most famous is Alton Castle which he built in the 12th century.

The neatly kept grass all around the Abbey ruins, somehow softens the hard lines of a building in decay. Standing some 40 feet high it must have been a marvellous sight to the peasants who tended the nearby fields. The beautiful arched windows would have looked out over green fields and the sounds of chants and prayers would have filled the air.

When the last Abbot, Thomas Chawner, left the Abbey in the mid 1500s, it did not take the local peasants long to use the building. The wooden parts, as they fell, were gathered by children, the herbs and vegetables from the gardens were eaten and the stone was taken away to be be used for the peasants' own farm buildings. With careful examination, the original stone can be seen in a farmhouse close by. It was many years before people would think it wrong to take away the stone of such an important building.

Although there is no Abbot at the Abbey now to keep the order of silence, it is still much easier to be quiet as you walk within the walls than

A Pint-sized History of the Staffordshire Moorlands

to talk. With nothing now to stop the elements the only sound heard within the walls is that of the song thrush as he looks for food among the bushes, and now and then a cuckoo. And as the evening sun begins to cast long shadows on the cloistered pillars and doorway, owls can be heard. Even after many centuries it is still possible to make out the former shape of the Abbey and with just a little help, lancets, transept and cloisters are identifiable. Even the monks' parlour can be found. Only there and perhaps in the dormitory is it, perhaps, a little easier to talk.

Nothing but peace can be found at Hollington and Croxden. Perhaps this is why the heart of King John is buried at Croxden. It has been said that monks from the Abbey ministered to the King before he died. After what was to be his final campaign against his rebellious people he was taken ill with a fever. Unloved by many of his people for his displays of luxury, it was hard for King John's men to find someone to care for their King. It was said that the monks from Croxden Abbey went out to Newark to tend him. There are other places which lay the same claim as this - one such place is in Leicestershire where there is an Abbey of the same name.

Peace and splendour can still be felt

After King John's death in 1216, his body was taken to Worcester Cathedral where he now lays in full splendour remembered by most for his part in the romantic tales of Robin Hood where even his soured mind and base actions are mellowed somewhat - perhaps rightly so, because if his heart is buried at Croxden, his soul must be now at peace.

CHAPTER 21
Isaac the gardener at the Linden Tree in Ipstones

Anyone who follows the road sign 'Ipstones' is going somewhere special. As soon as the corner which takes you into the village is turned, something happens to the landscape. Instead of an open countryside of stone walls, hedges and fields, there are sandstone buildings, whitewashed houses, grey-brown walls and the tower of St. Leonards Church dominating the view. This close knit community with its tiny cottages and neat gardens is a pretty Moorland village indeed.

Just as no large Staffordshire town is complete without a grand town hall so no Moorland village is complete without its friendly public houses. In Ipstones, according to the regulars, there none better than the Linden Tree. Nevertheless it is not just public houses which makes this village special. This village like many others in the area is made up of people and dwellings; not grand people like those whose memorials are contained in the 18th century church or lived in the many local manor houses; just friendly people living in small cottages.

Many of the old cottages in Ipstones, built before the village really prospered, and also many others built because of the iron ore found close by, have gone, but here and there, there are old parts of the village which remain as a reminder of a life which is nearly gone. Even though modern appliances and decor have standardised dwelling places in communities nowadays, a village cottage still feels very different from a town house. Outside the differences are even more noticeable. Town houses have concrete patios, container grown shrubs and gas-fired barbecues cooking American style food. A village cottage has its garden.

The village garden has always been an important part of the life of an Ipstones family. The gardens of the manor homes of this part of England had boxed hedges and formal rows of flowers neatly arranged. The main use for these beautiful yet often scentless flowers was large arrangements to grace elegant dinner tables. But with a cottage garden in a village like Ipstones it is different. Everything in a country garden has a reason to live. On the whole a cottage garden is an extension of a cottage pantry. Beans, peas, cabbages and onions all have there place alongside the more decorative plants. Lavender flowers not only look good in a front border but are just the thing to keep the moths away from the winter clothes. Angelica with its cream flowers and large leaves not only makes a sweet smelling plant but where would a plate of small cakes be without a decoration of crystalised Angelica on the top. Rosemary, thyme and mint are equally important in Ipstones.

The regulars who use the Linden Tree will always welcome visitors to the village with open arms, a wide smile and even a promise of a cutting from a favourite plant in much the same way as they have done for years. You see, they are well used to visitors at Ipstones, over the years this small village has seen a great many people come, go and return. Once this village has been visited it is impossible not to want to return again!

Everything in the garden has a purpose in Ipstones

Nevertheless some visitors are not seen as often as they used to be. Not too long ago, this village was well used by the travelling people who moved from town to town. Avoiding the main roads busy with traffic, they would use the quieter roads and call in to many of the small Moorland villages on their way. Today most of the travelling people who arrive in a town bring with them large trailers carrying all the paraphenalia of the fun fair and this makes it impossible to visit the smaller villages. They set up on a large open space for a few days before the wooden flooring is packed up once more, the waltzers stored in the large vans and the fair has gone.

This is not always how it was. In the years before the motor car was king and caravans were air-conditioned, the travelling people or as most of them would prefer to be called, gypsies, used real horse power to travel from Leek to Cheadle. Ipstones surrounded with the common land of Noonsun Common made an ideal place to pass a few days before moving on. True gypsies were, and still are, quite different from the people in the small villages they visit. In years gone by, proud dark eyed gypsy men spent evenings hunting in the nearby Massey woods and the days were spent trying to buy or sell horses outside the village Smithy, while olive-skinned women spent their evenings sitting on the steps of their beautifully decorated caravans in the open fields towards Ipstones Edge, making flowers to sell during the day to villagers. "Buy a flower for good fortune, Mrs" was often heard outside Beard's shop.

Gypsies like everyone else need to live. Food was essential for the gypsy family and what is now thought of as unappetising was in years gone by considered, with the addition of a few locally grown herbs exchanged for some wooden pegs, a tasty dish - roast hedgehog, squirrel stew and even rook pie were at one time normal dishes to be eaten with relish around an open fire.

Today even the most rural of village folk would not consider clay-baking a hedgehog in the embers of a wood fire or popping a jointed squirrel into a stock pot of freshly picked garden vegetables. The nearest most get to a gypsy meal is the occasional pigeon pie or rabbit stew, which, although not quite the same as rook pie is as near as an Ipstones person can get without offending anyone. Many a welcome tea has begun with the sentence "Warm that broth up Mother, Bill has come home."

CHAPTER 22
Kenny the cleaner at the Plough in Kingsley

Visitors to this Moorland village might well stand with camera in hand looking for things to capture of the life of a community long ago. They might think the best way to do this is to take a snap of the oldest buildings in the village and the first place they might check out is the public house. Nevertheless as anyone who is fortunate to talk to the regulars of the these wonderful buildings will soon discover, there are many places in a village which are older.

One of the favourite public houses in Kingsley is the Plough and it makes a lovely frame for any picture especially if locals are included in the snap. Nevertheless the buildings and its regulars are young compared with some of the other landmarks of the village.

A view of the thriving community of Kingsley

Granite faced old men with hands gnarled from years working in windswept fields, copperworks or mines, are only too willing to point their twisted fingers to buildings which are much older. After a while, as they talk, the buildings and people which they saw yesterday as they walked to the Post Office become confused with those which have long since gone. Somehow though it does not seem to matter.

One of the first things which can be noticed is that although the social life of many of these old men now revolves around the public house, they know just as much about the other buildings and people who have helped Kingsley to grow. Even without a camera, with the help of village people, a clear picture of a moorland community emerges.

Even the oldest of the regulars with the sharpest of minds can only talk about events, buildings and the people of Kingsley after the Great War but this gives a good picture of life in Kingsley and corresponds well with the old black and white picture postcards which can be picked up at collectors fairs. Conversations remembered from fathers and grandfathers give a small, perhaps faded, snapshot of Kingsley's history which is impossible to capture on film now.

As with other Moorland villages, life for as far back as any memory can go, was a mixture of good and bad and revolved around the church, work and the beerhouse. The good people of Kingsley would spend Sunday in the church or chapel and most of the rest of the week trying either to beat or avoid the rougher elements of the village life. What we see now as barbaric was considered quite normal in the 1800s. It is hard for people today to comprehend what is was like to live in Kingsley all those years ago. Take the case of William Collier a family man of Kingsley. This 35 year old father of 7 children was hanged at Stafford goal before a crowd of over 2,000 people including children. Whatever crime he perpetrated (it was in fact the murder of the local squire) was overshadowed by the fact that this man not only had to stand on the public gallows but he suffered the indignity and pain of a bungling hangman who had insecurely tied the rope. After the cheer went up ,as the rope tightened, instead of a quick end to his short life, poor William fell to the ground.

The crowd, now excited at the spectacle, hooted, and cried in one voice, "Shame, Liberty for the Kingsley Man." With a disregard for the roar of the crowd, the stone-faced officials were determined; there was no mistake on the second attempt!

Alongside this hardness of daily life, was church life. The rebuilding of St Werburgh's Church in 1819 which as far back as the 13th century had held services for the villagers, gave new life to the community. This grand building in the sight of the spire of St Giles Church in Cheadle and the sound of its distant peel, helped to give the village of Kingsley a little dignity back. So dignified is the view in fact that whilst in the area lyricist Fredrick Faber was inspired to write the words to the hymn "Hark Hark My Soul". He penned many other hymns but no words give such a true picture of this valley than ''Far, Far Away, Like Bells at Evening Pealing.'

The church was an important part of village life in the early 1800s. The impression most people had was the grander the building the better the people who attended. Over the years, St. Werburgh's has been attended by some of the most notable people in the area, many of whom left money to be spent on the building when their maker called them home.

But at that time, although God was their maker, most people still believed in evil spirits lurking in the dark corners of the churchyard. It is said that although there is a plausible explanation as to the fact that St. Werburgh's is a weeping church (that is, it tilts slightly to one side), the legend is that after the box pews were replaced in 1886 it so upset some of those parishioners who by then were residing in the churchyard that the great church bent its head just slightly to give them comfort.

St. Werburgh's was not the only place where the good people of Kingsley could talk to their maker. The Primitive Methodists had taken over the mill operated by Phillips of Tean in the early 1900s and built a chapel on the site to add to the Wesleyan Chapel which was by this time 100 years old. Kingsley was known not only for its church-going community at this time but for miles around it was known as one of the roughest places in the Moorlands, bare-fist fighting being one of the favourite 'sports' and considered one of the best forms of relaxation by the drinkers at the Plough Inn - although their enjoyment was looked on with much concern by those who frequented the Temperance Hall.

The village of Kingsley at the turn of the 20th century was quite large with the Kingsley Endowed School giving the young people a good start in life, although when the autumn hay-making season came, most of the children would miss school to work on the land with their family. A typical autumn day in the early 1900s in Kingsley would see the High Street busy with carts piled high with hay. Driven perhaps by inexperienced carters, these carts would take the corners quite slowly, while the 'experts' stood by the front of the Plough giving tips on driving. As Mr Sutton the Postmaster surveyed the straw that had landed on his shop frontage, old Mrs Cooper with her long dress and black bonnet, tut-tutted at the inconvenience of having to step round the deposit left by the horses. Although, these steaming deposits did not take long to disappear, for keen gardeners with buckets and shovel in hand would appear from the doorways to clear the hard core road.

As the evening light began to cast long shadows in front of the Plough. the lamp lighter would be seen. Gradually the gas lights were lit and an orange glow would bring the light back to the High Street. As with most villages, changes came to Kingsley. By the time the Shawe, the former home of the Lords of the Manor, was sold in 1919, Kingsley was changing fast. Today there is nothing left of the Shawe, no grand house, no gardens and pleasure grounds, no fish ponds; only memories and a few faded photos.

Nevertheless as long as at least one public house remains standing in the village, Kingsley will always have a history which for the price of a pint can be relived for a short time.

CHAPTER 23
Keen-eyed Biff at the Blacksmith's Arms in Kingsley Holt

To any one who passes through, it would seem that very little of the old village of Kingsley Holt remains. When Sidney Goodwin cut the first piece of turf out for the New Council Houses of Kingsley Holt in 1921, many of the older residents of the village thought that by the time the last of the 60 houses were occupied, the village they all knew would be lost in a sea of uniform houses and gardens.

With a weekly rent of 10/- these new houses brought a new type of villager into Kingsley Holt. Preference for the houses was given to members of HM Forces and their families and this meant that within a few years, the bar of the Blacksmiths Arms public house which had once been filled only with farmers, local traders and miners, was now occupied with soldiers and other uniformed men.

Tales of bare-fist fights at Kingsley Holt

Even before those councils houses were finished, changes were beginning to take place in Kingsley Holt. By the late 1940s only the memory of the old Primitive Methodist Chapel remained. But perhaps some memories are best forgotten like the fact that this tiny chapel built for the glory of God lived out its last few years as a chicken breeding centre!

One of the few things which has not changed is how the people use the Blacksmiths Arms as a place to meet and talk of old times and trades, although with even the older people losing the local dialect, only occasionally do a group of people talk in the true language of the Staffordshire Moorlands, which to many people even today is barely recognisable. The older generation of Kingsley Holt are getting few and far between, therefore it is especially good when tales are shared in the bar of the Blacksmiths Arms. The best time to talk to the historians of Kingsley Holt is late into a winter's evening when the warmth of the bar loosens the memories of times long past.

As the old man settled down into one of the chairs in the corner of the bar it only took a little encouragement to get his vocal cords lubricated. It was then easy to get him to talk of the old days and how as a young man he earned the money to keep his family fed.

Biff's features told of a hard life, the scars and lines making his face like a 3-D map of the countryside and one feature noticeable more than the others was his large mis-shaped ears. Once he began to talk it was evident that in his youth, to earn a little money, Biff had taken part in that most barbaric of sports - bare-fist fighting. For just the price of a pint he promised to tell the assembled group of one of the great local fights.

As he began to talk it was obvious that the tale he was telling did not happen in Kingsley Holt and was long before he was born, but somehow it did not matter. Because like so many good tales it does not matter about the location or the finer details. Before the froth from the mouthful of beer had been wiped away from Biff's wiry moustache his tale began.

Many years ago a fight had been arranged between one local man, Pickin Harvey, a 9-stone champion who earned his living going from one village to another fighting any contender, and his opponent, this particular Wakes Weekend, Joe Salt whose weight was touching 16 stone. When Pickin heard about Joe, his reaction was fear. "No way" said Pickin. But as a great deal of money had already been placed on the fight, Pickin began to think he had no other option but to fight. His trade was fighting and fighting he had to do!

After spending a lot time thinking about how he could get out of the fight, the day before the fight Pickin had a good idea. Due to the continued battering Joe had received over the years his vision was not as good as it once was and his brain was not as sharp as it might have been. So he hatched a plan.

That morning, off to Cheadle Pickin went and bought himself a secondhand suit three sizes too big. He then bought a sack of straw. On the morning of the contest he put the suit on and padded it out with the straw. As the two men walked into the ring before the fight Joe, with eyes squinting in the sun looked in horror at the sight of Pickin. "I am not fighting him." he screamed "That's not Pickin." With another shout he turned about, ducked under the make-shift ring and locked himself into to the nearest outhouse, vowing never to come out again. Now, due to the fact that Joe would not fight, Pickin was declared the winner!

After Pickin collected his money he moved out of the Moorland area because as he said he just might see Joe or one of his friends again and this time he might not have his special suit on!

As Biff came to the end of his tale his voice changed from his craggy words which were quite audible to the language of his father and grandfather which began to get less and less understandable. Words such as dunna, wunna and conna made the sentences harder and harder to understand and added to this, Biff's voice broke into great gales of laughter as he thought of the two men again.

By the time one more drink had been ordered it was pointless asking Biff any further questions about his fighting days or whether in fact either of the two men in the story were related to Biff. After a short while, Biff cleared the last drop of beer from his glass and the licensee called time. Biff buttoned up his gaberdeen overcoat and tucked his wool scarf inside the neck. There was no more time tonight and due to the passing time there might only be a few more evenings left to share with men like Biff and his tales. Every tale told by a local storyteller must be savoured because one day in the not too distant future these tales will only live in story books.

CHAPTER 24
Light nights Les at the Travellers Rest at Leekbrook

Whether coming from the large pottery towns or going to the small Moorland towns and villages, the area known as Leekbrook has little to make it look different from anywhere else and probably goes unnoticed by people passing on their way to and from the busy market town of Leek. But local people have always loved their area around the Travellers Rest public house with the two solid bridges spanning the ancient road.

When locals call into the low-beamed building of the Travellers Rest, filled with nick-nacks and comfortable fittings, the conversations they have with their fellow drinkers are filled with words and phrases that seem normal to them, but which visitors might find as strange usage of the English language. Take that simple question "What is the time?" "Five and twenty past one," comes back the answer. When questioned about this wonderful way of relating the time, local people would be unaware that 'normal' people would say the phrase in reverse order and if so questioned, the task of reversing the numbers would be laughed at. Most people think, the correct way to say the time is, 'twenty five past' but if traced back to the old records of 1066 the reverse form can be found. Even by the 16th and 17th centuries most works of literature still used what we call the reverse form of time, that of putting the larger number at the end of the statement.

Then when did it change? Could the natives of small compact areas who guarded their land with such ferocity against invaders from abroad, guard their spoken word and keep it unchanged throughout the centuries? Oh, no! Surely not our friendly country folk. With the generous nature which most of the residents of this wonderful land of ours had then, as now, they welcomed visitors. Slowly communities were altered by the various invaders as they passed through. One such group of people to pause in the Moorland area of Staffordshire were stragglers from Bonnie Prince Charlie's great army. These Highland warriors spoke in a language that was barely recognizable to local people. Gradually and without consciously being aware, their accents were picked up by local people. Over the years mostly due to the lack of formal education the way we spoke changed. Along with many other phrases, numerical figures relating to time began to appear in their present form.

But all this was a long time ago and is a history not often spoken

Ask them at Leekbrook what time it is

about in the Travellers Rest. When people visit these subduedly-lit rooms, the history they talk about begins well after Queen Victoria left the throne and when the motor car was coming into its own. At this time landowners and the gentry were the only people who had their own transport, most people relied on other forms of transport and one of the best known sights on this main road became a Berresford's bus.

The single decker bull-nosed buses took the farmer's wife and family out for the day. While many of those back-loading double decker's were used by the workers at the Paper Mills at Cheddleton. Every Berresford bus had seats of all colours and sizes and a bell that rang its message loud and clear. Each driver and conductor was known more for their individual character than their uniform and the bus itself had a passenger capacity that was beyond all credibility. Oh yes! A Berresford's bus was a sight to behold on the road to Leek.

Within the memory of most people aged over fifty, one of the commonest conversations that used to take place at the bar of the Travellers Rest, was whether Jimmy Berresford's bus would arrive at the bus stop for

"Five and twenty past one". This bus gave the working men just enough time for a pint of the best before the afternoon shift at the Paper Mill. This shift was considered one of the better ones by the workers. The shift disliked by most people was the night shift, with workers setting of for work when most good people were thinking of their last pint at the Travellers Rest.

One way to lessen the despondency of the night shift worker was to start work with a smile. What better way to create a smile than to play tricks on the young lads who were working their apprenticeship at the Paper Mill. Tales would be told of the spirits that lurked not behind the bar but on the road to Cheddleton. Perhaps there was a little truth in some of the tales but most were told just for 'fun'. Many a lad has been caught out by the tale of 'the disappearing passenger'. This 'old man' caught the bus outside The Travellers Rest at Leekbrook but never reached his destination.

The trick was quite easy to set up on a dark night once a young lad was sitting on the side seat of a double decker. After the other passengers with their haversacks filled with 'snapping' boarded the bus, on would clamber the 'old man' coughing and wheezing. He always wore the same old battered overcoat and hat and smoked an evil smelling pipe. With much effort and making sure the lad helped him, 'the old man' would ascend the stairs for a smoke. When the Paper Mill was reached the bus emptied and the young lad concerned about the old man's well-being would venture to the dark upper deck only to find the rows of seats empty and the old man nowhere to be seen.

With great glee the white-faced lad was informed that he has seen the 'Phantom of the Paper Mill', where as in fact what he had seen was one of his work mates dressed up, his haversack well hidden under the battered overcoat. With the lad back downstairs in his seat, the battered overcoat and hat were tucked firmly under the seat with the extinguished pipe, ready for the next unsuspecting lad.

Only memories are left now of the bus company and the paper mill, but the Travellers Rest remains, welcoming all types of people both young and old. Hopefully for a long time to come the words on their lips will still be, "It is still only 'five and twenty past' and there is just time for one more pint".

CHAPTER 25
Lil and her husband Dobbo at the Cattle Market in Leek

It was once written that England was a nation of shopkeepers; well what should have been said was that 50% of the nation were shopkeepers, the other 50% were market stallholders, because there is hardly a town in England which does not have a market. What is the difference between a market stall and a shop? Well, just visit the Moorland town of Leek on market day and find out. After calling in for a lunch time drink at the Cattle Market public house, take a walk along Derby Street. Each of the many shops have elegant window displays to tempt the customer, the glass-topped counters inside the temperature-controlled and carpeted shops have neatly uniformed assistants to smile and wish you a good day. Just the place to go to everyday. Well nearly everyday, that is, because there is nowhere quite like Leek on market days.

Most markets have now become artificial places with mock Victorian lights shining over mass-produced clothes. All the goods sold are dropped unceremoniously into gaudy plastic bags by the tradespeople who spend their lives going from one market to another, their large vans loaded with rails of clothes. Leek market is on the whole different. Nearly all of the stallholders are ordinary quiet people with a love of open spaces. Many spend most of the week working hard tending their animals and the land around their home but come market day they set down a pitch on the cold, age old cobbles within three feet of another stall. And the old Butter Market makes an ideal spot for Leek indoor market. This place once only sold dairy produce but now it sells everything from a birthday card to a new coat.

In recent years health and safety regulations have changed the way things are sold, even in markets, but in the heyday of Leek market, the stallholders were as colourful as the stalls themselves. Most of the outdoor market stalls in Leek sold farm produce of some sort. Few country folk in years gone by needed the luxury of new bedding neatly folded and packaged. What bedding was not passed down from mother to daughter, was made from off-cuts from the mill.

The market stallholders in Leek sold their wares in a way which has almost vanished now. Before electronic scales, heat-sealed packaging and fluorescent labels, came brass spring-loaded hooks attached to aprons and paper packages tied with rough string.

Market days are always special at Leek

As soon as the stalls were set up, often before the sun had fully risen over the distant tower of St. Luke's Church, first one voice then another could be heard. "Freshly skinned rabbits 6d each" or "Hares for sale today". If, before the sun begun to cast long shadows around the Challinor Fountain which until the early part on the 20th century stood by the Butter Market, there were any rabbits left, the sentence would become undistinguishable, the words changed from an audible sentence to just a jumble of sounds.

The well-built man in his late 60s on the corner stall of Leek outdoor market in 1890, was known by a formal name used every morning by the market official as he placed a tick in the market ledger book. But this gravely-voiced man was known to everyone else as Dobbo. A red-faced man with a white apron, which thanks to the addition of some off-cuts of tape was tied once at the back and then across his ample middle, sold all sorts of meat and poultry in Leek long before the fountain was moved. His talent for being able to produce meat for his stall when no one else could, gave him the nickname Dobbo from the fact many people thought even Dobbin the old farmhorse risked the chop if neccesary to make sure there was meat on sale.

To any one who knew no better, Dobbo was not known for his in depth conversations. Nevertheless once those glasses, which most of the time balanced on his balding head, rested on his face and the pencil stub came from his waistcoat pocket, Dobbo was a different man. With a lick of the pencil lead, on the smallest corner of a piece of paper, he could tell just how much his customers owed him within the time it took his wife to loop and tie a parcel.

Unlike most of the stallholders in the open market Dobbo would leave his wife in charge one afternoon a week. After a liquid lunch, Dobbo could be found in the old cattle market looking for a bargain. By the time his wife had sold the last of the meat on the stall and packed her belongings into the two-wheeled cart, Dobbo had chosen a least one cow to add to his small herd. With stick in hand he would guide his purchase past Cross Street towards his farm on the Ashbourne Road.

If you like the idea of being part of the history of the Staffordshire Moorlands, just call into Leek on a Wednesday Market Day. After spending some time in the Cattle Market Inn sharing a drink with the locals, walk along to the Market Place and buy something from the outdoor market. What you will take home is not just fresh produce, but a little piece of history will be yours.

CHAPTER 26
Light-footed Ginger at the Unicorn in Leek

Public house signs have always been special. One of the main reasons people visit a public house for the first time is the sign above the door. Arriving in Leek from Stoke-on-Trent, one of the first public house signs which take the stranger's eye is that outside the Unicorn Hotel, set squarely on the corner of Brook Street and St. Edwards Street.

The sign depicts as best as any sign can that wonderful creature the Unicorn. The Unicorn is a mythological creature with magical powers. It was said to have a sleek white body with mane and tail of fine hair but although the same size as a small pony there would be no confusng this beast with any of the ponies which until recent times used to take the well-bred ladies of Leek through the town centre in their small carriages to St Edward's church on Sunday mornings. Instead of small lace caps which on warm days kept the ponies' heads cool as they clip-clopped along Church Street, the Unicorn had one golden horn protuding from the centre of his head. It is said that anyone who sees a Unicorn and touches that golden horn will have wealth and happiness from that moment on until the end of their life. Perhaps that is why many of the regulars in the Unicorn Hotel can be seen so close to the picture which is on the wall over the fireplace.

Although the Unicorn Hotel has a title which gives the idea of an imposing drinking place with rooms of all sorts, it is in fact a small unassuming public house with just one room for visitors, but it welcomes visitors with a smile as warm as the fire which the regulars stand around on a cold winter's evening. Before the white head of the first pint of best bitter has gone down, the regulars begin to talk about the town they and every one else call the Queen of the Moorlands. Many of these people although loyal to their favourite pub will talk with affection of the other public houses in Leek. There has always been a great many for the people of Leek to choose from. A few of the favourite haunts of the regulars of the Unicorn have disappeared over the years along with one or two other grand buildings such as that majestic building, Leek General Post Office which once stood in St. Edward's Street and the Dutch-gabled Swimming Baths in Derby Street.

The many drinking places left vary in size from large imposing buildings like the Talbot Inn by the Smithfield Centre with its ornate monogram and the year of building fixed high on its front wall overlooking

A Pint-sized History of the Staffordshire Moorlands

the Nicholson War Memorial Clock Tower, to others sitting in the middle of the mainly pedestrianised town centre. The tiny Bulls Head is almost invisible to the world. Its windows and doors are tucked away among the shop fronts. The only thing which makes it identifiable from the other buildings in the row is the faded sign swinging overhead and the warm smell of fresh beer coming from the open door.

As regulars of the Unicorn Hotel talk, the visitor begins to realize that even though each of the public houses in Leek is well-loved and used, they all jostle for space in the busy town with each other. Nevertheless as the people who use the the Unicorn will tell you there is more to Leek than public houses. The shops, businesses and listed buildings make this town one of the most interesting towns to live in or to visit. Keen tourists to Leek will arm themselves with a trail leaflet to guide them on their day out. This gives them a wonderful way to start looking at the town which has been synonymous with

The Butter Market next to the Old Red Lion

silk since the 1700s. Yet ask any one who uses the Unicorn Hotel how to discover Leek and they will tell you one of the best ways is to slowly walk around, and now and then look up at the signs which decorate the the walls.

There are shop signs of all sorts and sizes which tempt people to step into shops which seem to have been untouched by the 20th century. Alongside these are wall plaques. Due to the hard Moorland weather with its cold rain biting into everything which stands in its way and winds which blow through the warmest shawls, many of the shop signs have been created in recent years, whereas almost all the wall plaques have stood the test of time. These signs speak loudly of a time long ago, some even before that celebrated architect William Sugden designed the National Westminster Bank and the Nicholson Institute. Look at the ones on the Almshouses, these eight houses dating from the late 1600s. Each one has a small plaque over the front door which gives the dwelling its own individuality referring to the families that endowed the houses. The larger sign on the gable end of the row gives details of the Almshouses and the rules laid down by Elizabeth Ash when she bequeathed the houses in 1696 - residents must not frequent the alehouses and not be men or married women!

This often brings a smile to the regulars of the Unicorn because of the stories of the ghosts who occupy both the cellar and the attic above the livingquarters. It is said there is a one, the ghost of a man who many years ago after fleeing Ireland and the potato famine, stayed in the Almhouses for a short time. Before he could be discovered he fled across the road to the Unicorn where he stayed for some time earning his money playing his violin and singing. Ginger always hoped that one day a snow-white Unicorn would arrive on the doorstep. Good fortune was not on his side. Late one evening after a particularly jovial drinking session he paid a visit to the toilets which at that time were outside. On his return he missed his footing and landed in the cellar. The poor man never recovered from his fall and was taken with the help of a piebald pony and small trap by his family of travellers back to Dublin to be buried.

It is not very often any ponies are seen in Leek town centre nowadays and there is probably little chance that a Unicorn will one day glide swiftly down Broad Street to bring good fortune to the regulars of the Unicorn Hotel but it does not matter. The regulars have a wealth of memories to keep them going for many years to come and providing the beer is fresh, the music is good and the company stays as friendly, what more could they ask for?

CHAPTER 27
Lottie and Bert at the Cheshire Cheese in Longnor

The Cheshire Cheese public house in the township of Longnor has welcomed locals with a smile as wide as any cat for more years than any one can remember. One of most picturesque of all the Moorland villages with gritstone houses and dry stonewalls, all held in by two of the most beautiful rivers in England.

Longnor, as it is now called, is an almost perfect picture with the River Manifold on one side, a delightful stretch of clear water which begins its gentle meander high in the moorlands and the dark fast flowing River Dove which it later joins, on the other to keep the village in its place. It has been said that this river so loved by great fishermen was so called, not as many think from the Anglo-Saxon word Duva, to dive, from the way the fast running water dives and dashes along its course, but probably from an old word which describes 'black river' so called from the colour of the water as it reflects the craggy hills which overhang it.

Looking out of the shining windows of the Cheshire Cheese when the sun is reflected on the other buildings in the village, it is easy to see why local hero Billy Billinge who was buried in Longnor Church grounds in 1791 at the age of 112, always came home. It is said he died less than 150 yards from were he was born in a cornfield. A potted history of his interesting life can be found inscribed on the headstone in the churchyard near the entrance to the church.

The village of Longnor is now just a small community with many of the locals calling into the Cheshire Cheese public house on their way home from work or from the market town of Leek. The only time it seems to get busy is when it is time for the famous Longnor Races. With jockeys perched precariously on two-wheeled contraptions there seems more excitement in Longnor than at any race day in the market town of Uttoxeter.

In years gone by Longnor was itself a flourishing market village. The weatherworn board outside the arched entrance of the market hall speaks loudly of a time when sheep and cattle could be seen in the village high street, along with many other things sold for the best bid of the day. Even before the market hall was built in 1873, Longnor like so many other villages had its small businesses selling everything the local people needed. Stalls and upturned carts stood in rows on the sloping cobbled streets selling

The famous Longnor Races

farm produce. As well as this many of the people who lived in the stone-fronted houses used their front rooms to trade from; bakers, butchers, dressmakers and druggists all earned a living in the front rooms of Longnor - even a doctor.

When a death happened in the family all that was needed to be done was to draw the window sheet across the small paned windows and sit the open rough wooden coffin on the table ready for the friends and relations to pay their last respects to the sadly departed. In between front rooms being used as a chapel of rest, there were well rounded ladies with long white aprons and hair neatly plaited who sold hand-made rag rugs backed with sacking, and bundles of sticks. Red faced gentlemen in dark suits stood by their scrubbed tables selling home-made brawn in small pots - only the best pigs' heads and trotters were good enough for Longnor people. In other houses old men with worn trousers tied up with string, sat by foot driven lathes mending shoes and selling nails, pots, pans and farm implements.

As well as these front rooms and the market place, there was one more place where many a good deal was set. What better guarantee of sincerity than a handshake in the bar of a public house? Until the mid 1800s one deal to be sorted out over a pint was still the sale of a wilful wife. A few old public houses still have a large hook attached to the fireplace. Many people think this hook is to hang a cooking aid on but no. This hook was to fasten a chain to, the other end of which would be tethered around a pitiful woman's neck.

In today's easy going society a divorce is as easy to get as calling into the local high street solicitor and filling in a few forms. In years gone by, in fact up until the first Divorce Courts in 1857, the only way to be parted from a wife was by a private act of Parliament which would cost £2,000. This amount of money was way beyond even the wildest thoughts of most of the Moorland farmers. Therefore as a wife was classed as a chattel, she could be brought and sold like anything else the farmer owned. The practice of selling a wife was as organised as any other sale with the husband first having to obtain a small ticket giving him the right to sell. He would then walk his wife around the village square attached by the chain shouting out her good points. When a price which was acceptable to both the husband and the buyer was agreed, the three people would then go to the alehouse to seal the agreement.

Although this may seem grossly unfair to the wife, it was in fact the only way available to be released from a unhappy marriage. With careful planning from the wife who would know about the proceeding long before market day, the buyer could in fact be the wife's lover!

All this is part of history now with even the mere mention of wife-selling raising a wry smile in the Cheshire Cheese public house. No respectable husband would dream of selling the thing which is dearest to him! A wife is a joy to behold and marriage is a wonderful institution. This makes a woman's place in the home safe and her ability to say what she thinks acceptable to all. Nevertheless before she passes judgment on her wayward husband, it is always worth keeping in mind the 18th century proverb, "Keep your eyes wide open before marriage and half shut afterwards."

CHAPTER 28
Marvellous Maz at the Lazy Trout in Meerbrook

Looking down the main street of Meerbrook most people will say nothing could ever change this delightful view of stone buildings and narrow lanes. Share some time with the regulars of the Lazy Trout public house and they will tell you a different tale. As with most public houses, gradually the talk changes in the bar from the latest increase in the price of beer to talk about old times. The phrases before and after come into the conversation in any public house. There is nothing strange about that, the visitor thinks, nevertheless this public house is different. Once regulars in the Lazy Trout begin to talk a realization comes over the visitor that locals are not talking about the war which took away the youth and innocence of England in 1914 or the war of 1939 which was to change the world for ever. The before and after event the regulars of the Lazy Trout talk about happened much closer than the mud-filled trenches of Belgium or the beaches of Normandy.

The event which changed the lives of many of the people of Meerbrook took place right on their own doorstep. The building of Tittersworth Reservoir changed the lives of most of the locals in some way. To lose things like the once pleasant walk over the fields through Hillswood to Ball Haye Hall, or the right to change your local drinking place from the Fountain Inn to the Lazy Trout because some city official just says so seems a threat to your very freedom.

Only those people born after 1950 can stand by the water's edge of Tittesworth Reservoir and hear the call of wildfowl and think just about the fish which live beneath the water line. Older villagers look across that stretch of water and hear the sounds and see the sights of village life. For even though most of the buildings were demolished before the water came, it takes more than a few million gallons of water from the River Churnet to obliterate parts of a village which took centuries to form.

Echos of that part of the village which was submerged have their roots buried much deeper than the trees which were replanted by the waters edge when the reservoir was completed. It is said that if you stand by the bank side of Tittesworth Reservoir on a summers evening as last orders are called at the bar of the Lazy Trout, the sound of clinking glasses and people ordering just one more pint of best mild, can be heard in the now submerged Fountain Inn, although it is must only be keen fisherman who choose the waters edge at night, in preference to the friendly bar of the Lazy Trout.

Just as nothing can compare after a long day's work in one of the clothing factories in Leek, with the thought of a cool pint of beer enjoyed in the delightful atmosphere of this Moorland pub, so nothing can compare with the though of a freshly caught trout for tea. Although, it can only be guessed at what that great man, whose name will always been linked with this fish which gives such great sport, would think of the trout being called lazy. For just as no one can mention Meerbrook without thinking of Tittesworth Reservoir, so no one can mention the name of this public house without thinking about the man whose name is synonymous with fishing. Isaak Walton is not just a hero of the north of England, his name spans the world, from the hunting lodges by the Great Lakes of North America to the city offices overlooking the River Darling in Australia, there is hardly a book shelf in the civilised world that does not have a copy of 'The Compleat Angler'.

Isaak Walton was born in 1593 and spent a brief time gaining an education in Staffordshire before going to London. It was to be 30 years before he was to return. His love of angling was intensified by the clear water rivers he found in North Staffordshire which he described as 'Some of the finest rivers in the world and most abounding with excellent trout and all sorts of delicate fish'. When he died at the grand age of 90, he left behind a legacy which will outlive the memory of an expertly prepared trout or even the most well preserved and mounted fish in a glass case.

Nevertheless when local people catch that silver backed fish with its streamline body and twinkling eye, they more often than not return it to its reed-lined home. For many local fishermen the thrill of the catch is why they sit by the bank side for long hours. Yet some fish are taken home for tea, even that ferocious looking beast the pike is classed as a delicacy in the Moorlands. Perhaps it is the thought of man competing against this wildest of creatures who inhabits the deepest of water which gives the pike its rich taste when it is served as a meal.

Whatever fish live in the hidden depths of Tittesworth Reservoir, Meerbrook people have a great regard for them. Because whichever water authority is in charge, the local people know that it is the fish who live beneath the water line who are looking after a very special part of their village.

A Pint-sized History of the Staffordshire Moorlands

What secrets of Meerbrook lay under this water?

CHAPTER 29
Osser the 'ammerworker at the Cricketers Arms in Oakamoor

Modern towns are built with straight roads leading from one place to another. Every good architect knows a good road is created first, then the homes and public houses. Long established communities are different, with little roads and lanes criss-crossing fields and sometimes even rivers. All the roads in a village seem to lead nowhere in particular. There is no hurry, they just meander along like a river, gathering buildings and people on their way. Each one of these tracks has its own unique twists, turns, bumps and history. This is what gives character to a village community.

The older the village is the more interesting are the things which can be found around every corner. The community of Oakamoor is like this. Even where local landmarks have long since disappeared, the memory will linger on much longer than the smoke from the big chimney at the mill ever did before it tumbled down in a great cloud of dust in 1963.

Although there is now little trace of the track where the railway once echoed with the rhythmic clatter of trains, many people still talk of them. The Toll Gate is still remembered by older villagers, while the land around the railway worker's houses is still called the Island.

The only real way to visit Oakamoor is to walk

The area where once Dr Bearblock and his wife Sarah lived in 1902 surrounded by mature trees and shrubs, some fully grown before the house was built in the 1700s, is still remembered fondly by some of the residents of Oakamoor as the Lodge. Other parts of this compact village seem to have been untouched by the passing of time. The road leading to the Cricketers Arms is a bit like that. Although not many people travel to the Cricketers Arms over Oakamoor Bridge in a two-wheeled pony mail cart like Mr Titterton did at the turn of the century, people still enjoy travelling at a slow speed in Oakamoor.

That is one of the things a visitor to the Cricketers Arms notices first when they call in for a drink. In the village of Oakamoor nobody seems to be in a hurry. Yet the working people of Oakamoor are known for their punctuality. For without it in the workforce of Thomas Bolton's Copper Works in Oakamoor, the laying of the first Atlantic cable would not have been completed on time. When the first telegraphic message was flashed from continent to continent in 1858, the people of Oakamoor were justifiably proud. Because without Sir Charles Bright trusting the workers at Boltons to meet the deadline, the copper core needed for the cable would not have been produced in time. Although by 1865 this communication was connected across the Atlantic, it was to be another 48 years before the first telephone was used in the village.

By the time that famous telephone call of Oakamoor had been made from the Copper Works to one of the local public houses, Oakamoor had quite a few established buildings of importance. The Memorial Free Church had been holding services for over 30 years, the railway station had been open for 37 years, while the two storey Holy Trinity Church with its square tower had held services for nearly 100 years.

In the 1900s, Oakamoor was a busy place and whereas many villages around still had gas lights to illuminate the streets, Oakamoor had an Electric Lighting Committee. Thanks to public donations the loan of £200 was paid off and the main street and even the Mill School had electric lights.

No one who talks about the history of Oakamoor in the Cricketers Arms can do so without mentioning the Bolton family. Their connections with the village goes back many years. When Alfred Bolton had a school for the workers' children built in 1871, he knew like many better factory owners of the time that a well-educated child becomes a better employee. The building of the Memorial Free Church in 1876 was a further attempt to create a good work force.

The Bolton family were hardworking and fair employers and they were well respected by most of their employees. So much so that when one of the Bolton family returned from his honeymoon, the people of Oakamoor decorated the streets with banners and a cannon was fired throughout the day to mark the event.

The Bolton family extended the already large house called Moor Court where they lived until it was bought by the Home Office in 1955 to be used for a few years as a Women's Correction Centre until it went back into privite ownership in 1983.

Nevertheless there is much more to Oakamoor than an old village and a few public houses, lanes and the memories of a great work force. Oakamoor is now part of a conservation area with people travelling for miles just to walk the woodland tracks. So next time you are out and about in the country, after walking among the trees and looking at the wildlife, head for the village, walk slowly down the main street and let the road lead you to to see some of the landmarks of Oakamoor. Just maybe the walk will take you into the Cricketers Arms.

CHAPTER 30
Old Owlface at the Jervis Arms in Onecote

Most people who live outside the Staffordshire Moorlands have trouble pronoucing the name of this tiny pub and the village which looks after it. It is said that it is possible to tell a tourist from a local person as soon as they say the name of either or both of them. In fact quite a popular game by some of the locals in the Jervis Arms in the summer months is to listen to the way visitors pronouce both as they share a drink with friends the bar.

A local will pretend to be another stranger to the village and will ask a visitor the name of the public house and the village they are in. Those people who know no better call either the public house, the Jervis *(Jarvis)* Arms or the tiny village One-Coat *(Oncut)*. After a sly smile most of the locals will agree that whether the public house is called the Jarvis Arms or the Jervis Arms is not as important as the village name, except perhaps, that is, to the descendants of the famous Admiral Jervis who was so important in the sea victory over the Spanish fleet. What local people will agree with is what the original meaning of the name of the village was.

The story behind the name will be recounted by any of the locals and it goes like this. When the Highland warriors passed through the area in the 1600s, some of the Scottish soldiers' job was to go ahead of the main party gathering what they could to help the army. As the main party spread out across the open land between Grindon Moor and Ipstones Edge, groups of them reached the tiny settlements along the River Hamps.

When these scouting soldiers joined back up with the main party they reported to their leaders of all the tiny hamlets they had seen. In their verbal report to their leaders they stated that some of the groups of dwellings they had come across on their travels had plenty of fresh water running through them with many groups of hovels. These they said were well worth visiting again as fresh supplies of food and clothing could be commandeered. Other settlements they said, had and only a few hovels but, some of these did have a Saxon Church with some things worth taking.

Other settlements like the community now known as Onecote had only one cote or cottage with nothing worth taking for the soldiers. It has been said that the soldiers stated that there was not even a decent winter's coat in the village worth taking to keep them warm in the biting cold Moorland winds.

The name given by some of Bonnie Prince Charles's soldiers all those years ago has stuck. Although very few local people would dream of calling their fondly-loved community anything other than 'Oncut'

All this gives the locals who use the pleasant drinking area of the Jervis Arms something to share with visitors who use the bar. Nevertheless once the history lesson has finished and the laughter at dialects has died down, the much loved side of the villagers of Onecote appears, talking about the village of today and telling visitors about the beautiful parts of this village. For although this village is still tiny it has some very interesting buildings. One of the most popular places in the village is the church. Many a new friend is found at the services or the beautiful Flower Festival held within St. Lukes Church, which was built in the mid 1700s

During the weeks before the Flower Festival something happens in the village. As the church slowly fills with flowers so the people of the village both young and old take an active part in the village tradition and as the weekend of the festival draws near, even the most relaxed of the people get slightly nervous. Will there be enough flowers? Will the displays stay fresh? Most of all, will people come to the village to share with locals the lovely creations.

Onecote Flower Festival is shared with all

What can be done to soothe those jaded nerves after a day struggling with flowers which will not go the way you want them. For many, a cool refreshing pint in the Jervis Arms is the answer. Yet what about those who through choice or age do not choose to sit by the bar of a public house? What do these people do when things get difficult and there seems no answer to a problem? For them and many more there are only a few things better than a pint. One of the best things to cure a problem, even if it seems as simple as a bunch of flowers wilting before they have been carried past the Jervis Arms, is to be found in the kitchen of a village house.

Because for people young and old, what can compare with a soothing jam sandwich? Nothing can compare with that pleasure to be found within two hand cut slices of thick bread from a freshly baked crusty farmhouse loaf spread thickly with best butter and a layer of homemade jam. Over the generations, people have shared this simple pleasure. Yet one of the local sayings in the village of Onecote is, 'If you have to go out on a moonlit night in Onecote, beware of the Indians who work the night shift in the Jam Buttie Mine!'

All the children of Onecote are brought up to know that beyond the safety of the gate which surrounds their tiny cottage garden lurks all sorts of untold dangers, none of which holds the puzzlement of why the Indians who work to create this favourite of all foods should be a threat. Nevertheless the threat is treated seriously by everyone.

The first question visitors to the village of Onecote ask when they hear the famous statement is, 'Where in all this beautiful countryside is this mine?' Well as locals know, that has always been a closely guarded secret. In fact so well hidden is the Jam Buttie Mine that it is said very few people have ever seen it.

Cynics will say the whole thing is just a tale made up by parents who like a pleasant way of keeping their children in check. Nevertheless those same people who do not believe in the Jam Buttie Mine and its workers would still think twice if someone warned them of the dangers of the 'Bogie Man'. Yet Indians who work creating something as marvellous as a Jam Buttie can not be all bad and must be better than a 'Bogie Man' who for no reason at all will consume small children just because they do not sleep at night.

Therefore for whatever reason you visit the village of Onecote, there are just a few things to remember. First the name of the village is pronounced 'Oncut'. Second, if possible visit the village when the Flower Festival is taking place, and lastly, but most important of all, 'Look out for the Indians'!

CHAPTER 31
Rusty the factory worker at the Crown in Rocester

Landmarks are important when travelling through an area and no more so than in the Staffordshire Moorlands. Churches, bridges, old factory sites, and the ever popular landmark when asking directions, the public house. They all help to give villages their individuality. Although nothing now remains, and perhaps rightly so, of that infamous Bug and Fiddle Inn which once stood between Lowlands and Crakemarsh, the village of Rocester has many other landmarks to make it special.

A drive out to the Crown public house in Rocester is a lovely thing to do at the weekend after a hard week's work. Although the Crown itself has quite a few tales to tell, Rocester's history goes back much further than either this or any of the other public houses in the area.

Long before the Bug and Fiddle served rough ale to the people who worked on canal barges and even before that ribbon of water, the Cauldon Canal, unwound itself through the countryside from Froghall to Uttoxeter in the early 1800s, the village of Rocester had already made a name for itself on the Staffordshire map.

The Romans knew the area well; with its close proximity to fresh water and open spaces it was an ideal base for their legionnaries. Barrow Hill where they set up one of their camps has yielded many Roman coins, pottery and a spearhead. This shows that the Roman soldiers used this area as one of their many camps.

After the Romans went, the area was left to nature again until a place of devotion was built in 1146. It can only be surmised as to why Bertram de Verdun who also had Croxden Abbey and the Abbey at Alton built, choose the area which was once called the Grange of Leys to have a Abbey in the area of Rocester built.

The modern visitor to the area travelling on the Uttoxeter to Rocester bypass can experience very little peace with traffic racing past. Nevertheless until this road was constructed the area near the 19th century church had, just like the Abbey at Croxden, little but trees, open fields and a true sense of peace.

After the dissolution of the monasteries, the site was taken into private ownership. One of the families who lived on the site in the 1800s was the Cavendish family. Of the many legends of Rocester, one which is often retold in the Crown is the Cavendish Curse, which said that while the house and land around Crakemarsh was occupied by a descendant of the Cavendish family good fortune would be with them, but, if for any reason the family were removed from the house, a curse was with them whereever they went until the very end of time, and those people who had the family removed would also be cursed.

There are many theories as to why and who bestowed such a curse on the family. Perhaps it had something to do with the activities which went on in such a once hallowed place or it could have been as simple as a travelling beggar being refused food and lodgings. Nevertheless many disasters were to befall the Cavendish family over the years. One which is particularly poignant was a much-loved member of the family who was lost when that ill-fated ship the Titanic went down. After the last of the family moved out of the house, the curse was not forgotten and for many years in the empty house hung a portrait of a member of the family just to keep the family at Crakemarsh Hall.

This part of Rocester's history is the side of village life people love to talk and read about. Most visitors think all the people who lived in villages like Rocester in years gone by spent their days either in the countryside tending the land and the animals or like the Cavendish family, hunting and shooting. This was not true and years ago a great many Moorland villages survived by the hardworking men and women being employed in the manufacture of goods to feed long canal barges transporting the goods to be sold in towns and cities.

Long sunny days in the open countryside was something which happened only in romantic novels and in weekly stories in the newspaper. Most of the people of Rocester lived their lives out working hard and only seeing open countryside on the occasional Church Sunday outing. Even before Mr Bamford began his work in a small lock-up garage in nearby Uttoxeter, the cotton mills were working hard to keep the village alive, although many of the trades of long gone days have disappeared now, with the names of the tradespeople nothing more than words in history books. They have been replaced by new trades at JCB, beyond the comprehension of people like Richard Bridden, who was listed as a cotton spinner in a trade directory of 1818, if he were to call into the bar of the Crown today. Yet just like the landmarks of Rocester, although no more, the trades of these first workers will never be forgotten. It is perhaps quite a fitting tribute to the people of Rocester that old and new are so close together and yet neither one outshines the other. Although the lasting epitaph to two of the great employers of Rocester could not be more different, both say without many words, so much.

The first is the thing that people cannot miss when they travel towards Rocester, the Fosser, a modern day giant born out of the family of earth moving machinery, the big and bold sign which tells the world the way to the JCB Factory. No intricate small plaque for this 20th century workplace. Once alongside one of the lakes with its metal birds, it would be easy to forget the village of Rocester. Yet within the time it takes to turn right and go over the old bridge, the other part of Rocester can be found, and on the wall outside the factory once owned by Richard Arkwright, a small plaque commemorates the place where the first cotton mill in Staffordshire was built.

The historic buildings of Rocester

Two places of employment for the people of Rocester, at first sight so very different, and yet separated by nothing more than 100 years and a small bridge.

CHAPTER 32
Ronny and his family at the Rudyard Hotel, Rudyard

Many people think a story is empty without the excitement of a mystery to punctuate it but in everyone's heart there is a quiet place with nothing but peace to talk about. To some people, the thought of this may be boring but when people sit by the windows of the Rudyard Hotel looking out at the trees what other way is there to talk than about peace. But Rudyard has got more than trees and a magnificent public house. It has the famous lake, a beautiful place where ducks gracefully glide on the water and shy animals still find solace in the wild grasses of its steep sides.

Since time began, man has loved places were the trees roll down to the water's edge, where the sun playfully dapples the ground, a place hidden from the outside world where peace is easy to find. Although this lake is man-made, this peace and much more can be found at Rudyard and the Hotel, even though it hides itself away. Once seen both lake and hotel are never to be forgotten.

The first mention of the community of Rudyard seems to be in Subsidy Rolls. The organised leisure pursuits seen around the lake today and the scantily clad young people with ice cream, seem a far cry from the hunting and shooting pursued by the Lord of the Manor of Rudyard with his tweed jackets and straw baskets of grand food. Upper class society at the turn of the century would spend whole weeks in the countryside living in luxury in their lodge houses overlooking the water, enjoying the peace of the clear waters of Rudyard just as much as the early morning coots. The young people of today can hardly spare an hour to enjoy the simple things in life. When older people speak of Rudyard it is the time in-between the Edwardian upper classes and the modern day they talk about.

Most local people spent Sunday afternoons at Rudyard Lake. Perhaps the best time was just after the war, when, even though money was scarce, people knew that the best place to take a small family on a 250cc Enfield with black sidecar attached, leather crash helmet and goggles firmly in place, was Rudyard with its lake. A magical place where the steamboats called across the clear water and city children gained innocent thrills in small rowing boats with views that could be marvelled at.

Only one thing spoiled those warm summer days of long ago and that was rain. For just as the checkcloth was spread, the hanky knotted as a sun hat and the Saturday Evening Sentinel rolled up to waft the wasps away from the tomato sandwiches, the dark clouds would cast shadows on the lake and a deluge would come! But not deterred by the change in the weather, out of the sidecar would come sturdy macintoshes to cover twin sets and black umbrellas to cover felt hats. Girls with pretty sundresses and fluffy boleros clutching small bunches of heather and boys with sleeveless pullovers and grey shorts with last weeks copy of the Dandy tucked into back pockets would gather under the skeleton of metal covered with a skin of Rayon.

After a while the older members of the party would began to answer the never ending questions which fidgety young children are famous for. Then would begin the stories. Some stories were based on fact such as the one about Captain Webb swimming the cold length of Rudyard. Other stories bent the truth just a little. Perhaps large pike did hide at the bottom of the lake but surely not large enough to jump out and gobble disobedient children if they walked off the pathways. Fig biscuits, fresh fruit and drinks of lukewarm tea from metal flasks would help to punctuate the tales until the rain had stopped and the picnic could continue.

Only rain stops the fun at Rudyard

More often today children spend rainy days enjoying the hospitality of the Rudyard Hotel itself while the rain makes rivulets of muddy water by the side of the boathouse, but even they tire of their Gameboys and tales still are told, like,"What a wonderful invention the umbrella is!' If it had not been for the philanthropist and traveller Jonas Hanway in the middle of the 1700s, we would not have this splendid form of shelter. The sight of him walking along the streets of England with this waterproof contraption was viewed with much concern and distrust, and it was stated by the clergy of the time that, 'Nothing should come between man and Gods natural rain'. It took almost 20 years before the humble umbrella was accepted in the cities and much longer in small rural communities like Rudyard but where would we be without it now?

But returning to our pre-war picnic, with the undivided attention of the children gained by father's tales, it would be now left only to one of older members of the group, more often than not a gangling youth who would much rather have gone off for the day with his mates, to shake his umbrella just enough to create a diversion and cause much squealing. as great drops of water dripped onto another unfortunate child!

Only time will tell if Rudyard Lake can survive unspoilt into the 21st century. Many families find it difficult to enjoy their own company let alone that of the lake nowadays. Added to this the water level is sliding down the marking poles at an alarming rate! But with the area being so much a part of family history, how can it be forgotten?

Just as a postscript or perhaps another tale - if Mr and Mrs Kipling had spent their honeymoon before returning to India, in one of the other small villages of Staffordshire, say Onecote or even Flash, would their son has been so pleased with his name?

CHAPTER 33
Rose, a new friend at the Knot Inn, Rushton

It has been said that the village of Rushton is a village in the wilderness. Perhaps, to an outsider, this looks true, but being in the middle of nowhere has nothing to do with a wilderness in the true sense of the word. A wilderness is something wild, untidy and unruly, which has nothing to do with the village of Rushton. This village with its delightful public house is made up of neat gardens and friendly people.

Long before Methodism was brought into the area and the tiny chapel built, Rushton was a thriving community. The Bridestones which are at Cloudside are said to be the remains of a Neolithic burial chamber. Perhaps they thought, like many people after them, that the higher the dead were buried, the sooner they would get to the promised land. By the time the Subsidy Roll of 1327 was written, the village of Rushton, or as it was called then Ruston, listed 12 people of importance in the village; this made it quite a large community for that time.

At the time of the White's Directory of 1851, the community was known by three names; that of the 1500 acres of land including the church dedicated to St Lawrence was Rushton Spencer; the 1000 acres in the manor of Horton was Rushton James; and the area which is now the centre of the village, Rushton Marsh, which included a Methodist chapel, a school, a railway station and three public houses. Most people now call the whole of this area by the River Dane simply Rushton and only occasionally the fuller title of Rushton Spencer.

Many tales are told to visitors to the Knot Inn public house and none more so than the ever popular story about Thomas Meaykin who was buried in the churchyard in 1781. This young man was born in the village of Rushton and moved to Stone to earn his living. When, much to the disapproval of his master, he fell in love with the daughter of the house, the master, quite a powerful man, had young Thomas drugged and buried alive at Stone. When the deed was discovered, his loyal friends opened the coffin to find it was too late to save poor Thomas who was face downward. They carried the lifeless body back to the village he so loved, and reburied him by the great firs and old yews.

Other tales are shared in the Knot Inn but few with as much feeling as this and few with so many endings. Some storytellers say that the girl so missed her love that she died not long after and is buried in Stone. Other say that she followed her beloved to Rushton and changing her name to stop her father discovering her whereabouts, tended the grave which had the epitaph: 'a man falleth before wicked men, so fell I' and lived her life out in a cottage in Sugar Street. The broken-hearted girl never married but was always known by the title of Mrs. It is said her ghost is one of the many who can be seen on misty nights in the church grounds.

The thought of this young girl wandering aroung the church grounds does not stop people visiting the ancient church of St. Lawrence. This unique church was built at least 600 years ago from local wood but had most of the timbers covered with stone in the 1600s when both the pulpit and the squire pews were installed.

All this architectural ingenuity, and built so far away from the village, gives it a beauty which is beyound compare. If someone talks about a visit to the chapel in the wilderness, don't be put off because once you have discovered this wilderness your heart will become so fond of it, you will have to return, like all those people who have travelled to it in the past by road or by the now disused railway line, you will never be the same once you have discovered this village.

A Pint-sized History of the Staffordshire Moorlands

People come from far and near to visit Old Rushton

CHAPTER 34
Sharky Sam at the Travellers Rest in Stanley

Finding a new public house is always a special feeling. When travelling along the A53, just one turn off the main road and it is not long before you find this very special public house, the Travellers Rest at Stanley. But what is it that brings all the people who were not born within the area of Stanley off the main roads to this tiny part of the Staffordshire Moorlands.

One of the many reasons strangers visit Stanley has nothing to do with the sign over the door of the Travellers Rest or the clear cool beer which is served everyday in the bar. It is water. Not the man-made Caldon Canal, with its neat sides no more than ? feet wide at water level and 4 feet 6 inches deep. No, it is open water and a place where strong winds blow across the blue green water and small waves and swells are formed.

Even though the the Travellers Rest is more than 90 miles from the sea, no one seems the slightest bemused when the talk in the bar takes a nautical turn, for not far away is that stretch of water, Stanley Pool, which calls people from all over the county to the water's edge.

Posh people on Stanley Pool

After a few hours wrestling with a stubborn boom and full blown sails catching the cross winds that blow hard across Stanley Pool, thoughts soon begin to reach further than the wooden landing stage. What better way

A Pint-sized History of the Staffordshire Moorlands

to relieve tight muscles and moisten wind-dried lips than a pint of best bitter in the Travellers Rest? There is another good reason, of course, and that is if the weather is unsuitable for sailing; if storm clouds are forming towards Mow Cop, few sailors will venture further than the bar anyway.

Most people take the extremes of weather for granted and only take notice when a mention is given about care driving high-sided vehicles or a hosepipe ban comes into operation. But in places close to sailing water, people are more aware of the extremes of weather. After a few weeks without rain, the older regulars at the Travellers Rest will start talking about ways to make it rain. Many of these are looked on as laughable by city people but most have been passed down from father to son and are said to have been used in country places for years.

One way to make it rain in Stanley, it is said, is to call for the rain clouds to come. The first thing to do is to gather a small group of people around a tin bucket with some water from Stanley Pool in it. After dancing around the bucket a few times the leader of the group should fill his mouth with some of the water and spit it into the air to imitate rainfall. The bucket is then turned over and the water allowed to spill onto the ground. The dancers then try to scoop up the water with their hands and fill their mouths with it. The rain dance then ends with all the dancers spitting the water into the air.

The cure for the other extreme of weather is perhaps not as hard to swallow but equally as strange. Everyone is welcomed in to the Travellers Rest including the occasional pet - and one animal is given a special welcome if it wanders in. An even bigger welcome awaits this animal if it is seen near the sailing yard full of boats, their covers fastened tight and their masts creaking in the breeze. The animal is a tortoiseshell cat!

Every seafaring person knows that a tortoishell cat foretells the approach of storms. If, when the cat is seen, it is sent to a high place it will frighten the storm away and the boats can be used again on the water. Not surprisingly then, it is not unusual for a tortoishell cat to be seen by the bedroom windows of the low-roofed Travellers Rest public house when the weather has turned grey in Stanley.

When the door of this public house opens, no matter what the weather is like, everyone is welcomed into the bar. Only occasionally a slight ripple in the conversation occurs and that is when one of the locals turns up in their Sunday best clothes in the middle of the week. After the first round of drinks, it does not take long before one man will be brave enough to ask the question "An' where dost think they are goin' all Nobby and Posh?"

Although this seems a normal enough statement, if you think about it, both words at the end of the sentence somehow seem as though they are not really part of the English language. There has always been words to describe people with money. One of the oldest is the word Nob or Nobby. Originally this word was a derivation of the word Noble from the latin 'nobilis' which in turn came from the word 'Nosco' meaning to know. The shortened Nob word became popular in the 18th century to describe the gentry of the day as they walked around the cities with their top hats and ebony walking canes. The more ornate the handle of these walking canes, the richer the man who carried it. At first they would be described as noble men, then gradually the word was shortened. Therefore, perhaps to describe a well turned-out person we should use the term, a Nobby person?

It was not until the 1920s that the other word ''posh' became popular though. But why do we use this strange word to describe a smart person. It was probably invented many miles away from Stanley by the office clerks in the great shipping offices of Liverpool and Southampton. When the new well-off booked their passage on ships, they of course wanted the best possible cabin. As everyone knows the best way to travel was and will always be (to avoid the heat of the sun), Port side of the ship on the Outward journey and Starboard side Home. The poorly paid staff in the booking offices were not impressed by these travellers nipped speech and often made comments about them as they left the buildings and one phase became common, first, behind the counters and then in the homes of the workers. When describing a well-off person, the workers used the first letters of the words they used to book these travellers - P.O.S.H. Gradually the word spread to become part of the language we use today.

Not that anyone who uses the Travellers Rest thinks such detrimental thoughts about visitors who call into the bar. So the next time you are looking for a nice place to visit, call into this public house and spend some time with some very posh and nobby people.

CHAPTER 35
Suave William at the Sportsman in Stockton Brook

If any public house suits its name it is the Sportsman at Stockton Brook. Set on the main road, its windows and doors, like every good sportsman should, survey its surroundings with an unbiased option. This public house is a place of refreshment for sportsmen of all sorts - and sportsmanship can be linked with all types, from the good to the not so good and what better type of person to use this public house than a good sportsman?

The Sportsman always welcomes strangers

Even good sportsmanship falls into many different categories. There is the good sportsmanship of the man who enjoys nothing better than to stand on the edge of a white-lined pitch and share with like-minded people a good game of cricket. With oiled willow bat cracking on neatly stitched ball, what better way is there to spend a summer's afternoon than in this most English of games? Or then again, there is the sportsmanship of those who from the comfort of an armchair or a bar stool will talk to any one who will listen. With great accuracy, this sportsman can gauge the angle and flight of the ball as soon as it is struck even though the game is played many miles away and the view of the pitch thanks to a television screen. These and many more experts can be found in the Sportsman public house.

Although not a regular of the Sportsman and not even a native of Stockton Brook, the old man sitting in the corner of the bar with a glass of the dark rum somehow typified all that a Moorland villager should be - smartly dressed and with a friendly smile. As the warm summer afternoon sun filtered through the windows of the public house, the old man seemed to somehow melt into the corner. There was nothing to distinguish him from any of the other old men who use the Sportsman as a reading room on a Saturday afternoon. That was until he spoke, his voice was as smooth and velvety as his glass of rum.

After a sip of his drink, he explained how he was to be found in a small Moorland pub on a sunny afternoon. His family he said were visiting the area from their native Ireland and were staying in a large hotel near Leek. Tired of bargain hunting in antique shops in Leek and armed with a map, a packed lunch and an all day bus ticket, he was out to explore. As the bus stopped for a group of young people to get on, he noticed the sign which said 'Village Barber This Way.' Without a second thought he got off the bus and not realising the sign was quite a way from the barber he found himself in the Sportsman public house, Stockton Brook.

With just the slightest encouragement and the promise that there would still be time for his haircut before the last bus back to Leek, he accepted another drink and proceeded to talk about the love of his life, cricket. Back home in his village in his native Southern Ireland, William Charles had been well known as a batsman for many years. With great clarity he talked for an hour about some of the greatest matches he had seen. From visits to that great Oval cricket ground were he watched white-clad players in front of large crowds, to tiny matches where he batted on village greens watched by only a few people between their talking and snoozing in the sun. He had an anecdote for them all.

William Charles said in his warm Irish voice that cricket was like the game of life with the bat being the opportunities we are given. We are all the batsman using our strength and skill to decide which is the best way to play the game with the final decision left to the Greatest Umpire of all. As the conversation progressed he spoke about cricket being one of, if not the greatest, game invented, and the most important person in any match, the umpire. This game, he said, was played and commented on in large towns and small villages throughout the country long before the invention of televisions with action replays and freeze buttons to sort out the validity

A Pint-sized History of the Staffordshire Moorlands

of a wicket. For no matter how clear the picture on the screen is, or whether it it has been caught on one or more cameras, nothing can ever replace a good umpire.

As time passed William Charles began to get slightly agitated and emptied his glass with his hand covering the glass top as if to prevent some one slipping one more rum in. "Hair to trim and the bus back to Leek to catch," he said. The walk along the road to the barber shop was punctuated by more comments about cricket and life.

Once inside the barbers, he took off his jacket to reveal a neat double breasted dark grey waistcoat from the pocket of which, just like the white rabbit in Alice in Wonderland, he produced a large pocket watch. With great ceremony he checked the time and returned the watch to its place. As the white cloth was placed around his ageing neck, William Charles commented in his mellow voice that although his bus was due shortly, and he needed to call into the little paper shop which reminded him so much of the railway station near his home, he still needed a good short back and sides. The barber obliged as best he could with William Charles's animated conversation never stopping for a minute!

After three more stories about cricket and a few barbed comments about how much of the sportsmanship of years gone by had disappeared even from this most civilised of games, a large soft white brush was taken from the barber's top pocket and gently swept across William Charles's shoulders. After being helped on with his jacket and bidding a fond farewell to everyone, he was gone.

The bus sailed past the Sportsman shortly after and a wave of a the Evening Sentinel could be seen from the road. William Charles was gone, probably never to be seen in the area again. Nothing was left of the day the great cricketer and raconteur visited Stockton Brook, except a fond memory.

CHAPTER 36
Tug the old teacher at the Cross Keys in Tean

Without doubt all those people who now use the cosy rooms in the Cross Keys in Tean have spent more than a few years at school learning to write neatly. Many of regulars in the pub began their education at Greatwood Primary School in Tean or as it was known until 1939, Tean Council School.

Who of them would have imagined that those small boys of long ago, who sat for what seemed endlessly long days in formal rows of desks reciting times tables and cutting their names inside the wooden desktops, would ever spend more than five minutes in a week with pen in hand now? Even those boys who chose manual work in the mills, still find they use the skills they reluctantly learnt all those years ago.

How many of these men who now spend time choosing where to carefully place eight crosses on a football coupon, think about the crosses emblazoned in red ink in their schoolbooks long go? As one more pint is ordered from the bar, the enthusiasts around the table talk of football tactics and recent performances of their favourite team. Before they place their crosses on the paper, one member of the group begins to doodle on a beer mat. After filling the border of the beer mat with crosses, the question is asked, "Has anyone ever thought about why two lines when straight are called parallel, but when one is moved on top of the other in a certain way it makes the mark known as a cross?"

Someone suggests the best thing to do is ask the licensee of the Cross Keys for the use of a dictionary. Hopefully this will answer the question and the filling in of the coupon can continue. Or will it? In the Oxford dictionary there are over 50 meanings for the word cross and each has quite a tale to tell. One of these must answer the question.

First the medieval entry: In those times to guarantee the sincerity of their intentions people solemnly kissed their signature in a gesture similar to putting ones hand on the Bible when taking an oath. Because of lack of formal education most people signed documents with a cross - thereby giving the logic to the fact that a cross is known worldwide as a kiss because a kiss finalised and bound agreements.

Many important letters have been signed over the years in Tean with a cross but none could have meant as much as those letters from girls who would stand on the steps of Steel's Post Office planting just one more

Learning to write at Tean School

kiss on a letter for their young men who had gone to fight in the Great War.

But a cross as a kiss is a good mark. One of the other meanings must be the opposite but how and why. Perhaps if the origins of that other universal mark is found then the origin of a cross as a failure can also be discovered. A tick (not often seen on a piece of work from a rebellious school boy in Tean who would have preferred to be in Temple Wood rather than in a classroom) stems from the word tic meaning a twitching movement of the body and was the obvious symbol to use for the slight pen movement on a written piece of work to acknowledge something having been read. Well if a tick marks the paper as being read, then once a line was struck through the tick it was obvious that although the work had been read it had not been passed as first class. This mark is the one that is remembered by so many people who were educated in Tean and says "I have personally checked this work and found it wrong but am unable to use my full signature every time I see a mistake."

When people talk of education in Tean, they talk with affection about Greatwood School. This was first known as Tean British School and was built in 1856. The teaching techniques of today seem very relaxed in comparison to those lessons before the 1960s. Copperplate writing was expected from very young child with any ink blots marked with the much dreaded cross by the teacher. This school replaced the much smaller building J.& N.Philips the mill owners had erected in 1810. The stern-faced teacher of that school would expect nothing but the best from the children who were lucky enough to go there but with sandtrays and slates to learn to write with, the children saw few crosses on their work.

Education years ago was only for the few though. Up until the turn of the century children were expected to work hard in the manufacture of tape, the product which gave employment and life to the area. For many years, even the smallest of children would be expected to help their families in weaver's houses like those which from 1798 until 1966 stood in Cheadle Road. As the call for tape increased, Philips Tape Factory was built in the High Street in 1822 and there was no better workforce to complete those orders from all over the country than the children of Tean.

All this has altered now with the young people of Tean expecting more out of life than 2 shillings a day and a Sunday School trip on a wagonette. Nevertheless some things never change. From working hard in the mill and putting a cross in a ledger book when collecting your pay, to buying and selling property in Tean, meant prosperity. Now a simple set of crosses chosen leisurely in the comfort of the bar of the Cross Keys, placed in the correct order, can lead to stocks and shares and holiday homes on Greek islands!

CHAPTER 37
Tubby the trailwalker at the Mermaid, Thorncliffe

Only complete strangers to the area would question the strange name of this public house; most people take it for granted. Few sailors, nevertheless, would find it comfortable this high up and so far from the sea, although one seafaring person has called this spot home for hundreds of years. The voice of the beautiful mermaid of Thorncliffe can sometimes be heard on misty nights and her home is that bottomless mass of water called Blakemere.

Very few people have seen this golden-haired beauty and even less have lived to tell the tale. It is said that she has been known to call out a welcome to unexpected travellers and with a wave of her delicate hand, they have joined her never to be seen again. But who is she, and why does she live such a lonely existence? It is said that all is not what it seems, lonely she is not and solitary certainly not. The following explanation has been passed down from father to son with its authenticity being lost in the mists of time that are as heavy as those that settle on the nearby memorial stone to rambler and world traveller, Paul Rey.

As one of the many daughters of King Neptune, the Mermaid of Thorncliffe once lived with all the other mermaids at the bottom of the sea. Along with her sisters her job was to sit on rocks in the warm waters of the Pacific Ocean and lure unsuspecting sailors into the watery depths to help to populate her fathers underwater kingdom. For as everyone knows, only mermaids are born, mermen have to be created from sailors. The job of enticing sailors was enjoyed by most of the mermaids. Nevertheless just occasionally a mermaid found the work, and the hot sun and salty water, too uncomfortable and this is how it was with the Mermaid of Thorncliffe. She would spend as much time as she could looking for caves to shelter in.

One day while out exploring, she ventured away from the others to find herself a cave. Once inside a strong current carried her past rocks of every colour and shape into a cavern, then along twisting passageways upward she was swept, until after many hours twisting and turning, her golden hair tangling around her delicate features like seaweed around a shipwreck, she saw a bright light which almost blinded her. Lifting herself onto the water's edge, she sat sunning herself, her pale eyes not able yet to focus.

Like most winter's days, the mist from the Buxton Hills had coated everything with a damp blanket of cloud and the mermaid spied what she thought was a group of mariners on a small vessel, their cloth caps looking remarkably like those worn by sailors. It was in fact a team of drovers taking packhorses loaded with fine china over the moors. Eager to please her father King Neptune and not realising she was many hundreds of miles from the sea, she called out to them. The drovers were so bewitched by her beauty, they followed her into the bottomless pool.

After the long journey to the bottom of the sea it did not take the drovers long to overcome their fears, they soon began to live happily in the underwater kingdom. Their packhorses were exchanged for gold at one of the great trading days which Neptune had with the Lord of the Amazon. As for their loaded panniers of fine china, the drovers used these as currency to buy two of the only things they missed from above, a plug of chewing tobacco made from the finest seaweed and a glass of beer brewed from underwater plants. What fine banquet dishes china from the Potteries made. King Neptune was the envy of the underwater world!

So pleased was Neptune with his daughter that he allowed her the freedom of the sea and no longer did she have to work with the others

Only the brave venture close to Blakemere pool on a misty day

enticing unsuspecting sailors. She had the choice of all the oceans in the world to swim in and yet, with all this freedom, all she ever chooses to do is to visit again the dark pool on the moor. The fresh air of the Buxton Hills has no trace of the hot salt air which burns a mermaid's pale skin and bleaches her blond hair. Blakemere pool has become her favourite place.

To this day when the damp mists hang low over the moors, she still sits and looks out over the Cheshire Plains to the Welsh Mountains. Her time is mainly spent combing her long hair and singing and although many people say her song is just the wind whistling around the low stone walls, occasionally she still uses her charm to invite someone to her home under the sea, to meet her father. So, the next time you fancy a short walk after sharing a drink with the regulars at the Mermaid, try to stay away from Blakemere Pool and on no account wear a sailors hat!

CHAPTER 38
Toots the storyteller at the Highwayman at Threapwood

Most of the customers who use the Highwayman in Threapwood now are young people looking for a good night out with lively music and flashing lights. Some of the older residents of this mainly farming community recoil in horror as they catch sight of the outfits worn by these young people as they clamber out of cars and taxis in the car park of this once quiet drinking place.

To the older residents of Threapwood, the sight of a group of shaven-headed young men with leather clothes, fills them with as much fear as any stranger dressed so differently would. As these same people look tactfully away from the visitors of today, they look at the sign which swings outside the building. They see on this sign another style of clothes. But the flamboyant clothes and manner of Dick Turpin portrayed on the sign and in the films and story books, gives a somewhat false image of highwaymen. Whether in fact Dick Turpin ever travelled the lanes around Threapwood or tied his sturdy Black Bess to the fences outside the public house, it makes a charming if far-fetched story to while away a few hours.

Nevertheless, there were at one time highwaymen who did earn their living by stopping the travellers who used the lanes and tracks around Threapwood. Many visitors to the area will think that this one-time local drinking place and staging post was given its name as perhaps a warning to would be travellers about the dangers which lurked around Counslow Plantation. But no! The name of this public house is in fact quite modern. It was not until the 1960s that it was called the Highwayman. When it was given its new name, it was also given a completely new image. Although this was to bring a look of dismay to many of the older people of Threapwood, the Highwayman gave young life to a very old public house.

Of all the other types of outfits seen around Threapwood in years gone by, perhaps one of those which stands out most was the outfit worn by the soldiers of Oliver Cromwell's Army. With no one left to give first hand evidence of any event which took place in Threapwood in years gone by and the fact that very little documentary evidence exists, it is left to the storytellers of Threapwood to retell the tale.

This tale was told with eloquence by a friendly local man known by one and all (for reasons too complicated to explain) as Toots. Mainly because of his age, Toots now finds other places to share a drink with his friends than the Highwayman whose welcome is to far younger members of the population. As the mellow colours of autumn are reflected in the small pools around Threapwood, Toots can be seen walking home along the lanes. With a glint in his eye and a smile on his face, he will willingly talk of how soldiers from Cromwell's Army dragged heavy cannons along the lanes of Threapwood to high rocky vantage points and how, with great skill, these cannons were aimed at the castle at Alton.

Only friendly travellers use Threapwood lanes now

Depending on the amount of liquid refreshment taken, the end of Toots's story changes. Sometimes the story ends with a tale about how a cannon ball missed the castle and landed just outside the village of Alton where a member of Toots family tried to drag it to his home with the help of a two wheeled truck. One of the hills close by the village of Farley proved too difficult and the cannon ball was allowed to roll into a nearby stretch of water. As a mark of respect the hill still bares Toots family name.

All this happened many years before Toots was born, of course, but it does not stop him telling the story with as much enthusiasm as if it all happened last week. Although there is little written documentation regarding the area, one of the important documents in the history of the Highwayman describes when the Green Man public house as it was called then, was sold as part of the Earl of Macclesfield's Estate in the early 1900s for £875. At that time it was just a place were farmers went to after a long day tending livestock. No fancy clothes were seen in the bar in those days! The best dressed farmers in Threapwood in those days wore heavy boots, old corduroy trousers held up with broad braces and fastened with buttons to leather loops, and a collarless shirt. This sight if seen today in the Highwayman would only raise a few eyebrows even from the young people. Nevertheless a few of the farmers in the 1900s would wear clothes which today would make most people flinch. Mole skin trousers and waistcoats were still being worn by the older farmers of Threapwood even until quite recently!

But when farmers of Threapwood brought their pony and trap out of the stables, they dressed in different clothes to pay a visit to market, either the small Cheadle market on Fridays or the large ones at Leek and Uttoxeter on Wednesdays. A smart Threapwood farmer would wear a broad pin-striped suit with matching waistcoat and often a spotted muffler smartly tucked into his open-neck shirt and a flat cap.

For Sundays, when he took his wife and family to church or chapel, and other important days, to add to the suit there was an ironed shirt, and out of the top drawer of the bedroom tallboy came a stiff white collar. Then came the skilled job of fastening the collar to the shirt. First the mother-of-pearl back collar stud was attached to the collar and shirt, then the front one was fitted. Only when this was done, and the armbands and cufflinks and a smart bowler hat were added, would the journey to church be undertaken.

Since the days of horsedrawn carriages taking people along the lanes has gone, and with the Highwayman bringing different types of dress and carriage to Threapwood, it would be easy to be put off visiting the area but one thing can be certain, a great many friendly people still use the lanes of Threapwood now.

CHAPTER 39
White-haired Wiggy at the Greyhound in Warslow

If asked to draw a picture of a Staffordshire Moorland village, almost everyone will immediately draw a few houses held together by stone walls with rounded tops and here and there a wooden gate leading to a small house covered with ivy and honeysuckle. And not far from this they would place a post office.

The post office in Warslow

If asked to describe more about what they have drawn, they would say, "Inside the house there will be a large clock on the wall of the parlour ticking away the minutes and chiming the hour, while the kitchen will smell of warm apple and cinnamon pies".

If asked to continue they might say "Outside the post office would stand a water trough for tired horses, while inside a plump softly-spoken lady would stand behind a wooden counter. This lady would be able to deal with any problem that occurred in the village, from sending a telegram to some far off place, to producing from under the counter anything from a magazine to a yard of pink ribbon to tie up a birthday parcel".

Warslow is that very illustration of a Moorland village with the Greyhound public house as a backdrop. Fiction stories of long ago in the 1800s might be set around a village such as Warslow. When the hero of this romantic novel rides out of the village into the night after being involved in some terrible argument, it could quite easily have been the son of one of the farmers of Warslow, fleeing from the wrath of Reverend William Richardson, the curate of the village at that time.

After bringing disgrace to his father and the village by wronging the daughter of one of the village gentlemen, there would no welcome for the handsome young man in the newly built church; never would he pray or sing hymns in his fine voice as the sun glinted through the new pre-Raphaelite stained glass window. So after calling into the Greyhound and gaining sustenance from a pint mug and the words of wisdom from the landlord, our young hero would ride off into the night.

Sometimes the story ends there with the girl staying at home to live her life out with her shame and a broken heart, but if the novelist has a soft heart, the hero might ride back and leave with the girl's arms tightly around her beloved's waist as the horse gallops faster and faster towards Hartington, leaving behind a red-faced father! Although by today's relaxed attitudes, stories like this seem nothing more than a fanciful tale, many young people in times gone by were subject to a very formal life and suffered terribly if they broke the rules.

This did not mean village life was never fun. With no cars on the roads until the turn of the century, the lanes around Warslow were playgrounds for the young. Pinafored girls and young boys played together outside the Greyhound, only occasionally to be chased away by landlords such as Thomas Wood, when it was off to other places where even better games could be played. Of all the popular games of that time, perhaps the game hopscotch involved the most skill. This was often played out on one of the few cobbled areas of the village. One of the problems drawing out hopscotch on rough ground is that the chalk does not draw the way it is intended on cobblestones and the numbered squares were often not quite as they should, but no one complained.

The small children either in bare feet or heavy boots, hopped from one square to another trying hard not only to jump the square with a stone in, but also not to scuff bare skin, or even worse, boots against the bare cobbled ground! Woe betide any child whose mother had to take scuffed shoes to Mr Barker the shoemaker before they were outgrown.

The game of hopscotch is still sometimes played today but one game which has altered beyond all recognition involved calling into Mr Beswick's, the village butcher's shop and asking for some small cooked bones often left over from the freshly made brawn he was well known for. These bones were sorted until five of just the right size were chosen, (the others were discarded to be gnawed on by the village dogs) and a small rubber ball was then produced and the game could get underway. The object of this game was to throw the bones in the air and then bounce the ball and collect as many bones off the ground as possible before catching the ball.

Of the other games the children played under the watchful eye of Mr Grindon the grocer, as he arranged his produce outside his shop, there was one which even after the passing of time still leaves a mystery as to the rules and the object of this game. It was always popular with the children of Warslow. The game, if can be called that, involved nothing more than standing upside down, against one of the outbuildings of, say the Greyhound, and firmly placing feet on the wall. Despite the fact that there was never any winners or losers in this game, it was always very popular.

If after being thus pestered for some time, Mr Wood grew tired of the sound of children playing, with a swish of a brush he would send the children running down the lane. This did not bother the children too much as the village had lots of places where adventures were to be found like in and around the many small buildings dotted in the fields around Warslow.

These small buildings made ideal castles. Doorways covered in nettles could be entered with the help of a jacket spread on the ground to press the stings away from bare legs and if one nettle managed to escape the jacket there were always plenty of dock leaves to turn legs green and relieve the stinging. Stones were easily arranged into eating and sleeping areas while windows looked out into open fields of sheep and cows which became something quite different - a battleground. Hundreds of soldiers clad in shining armour could be seen on the horizon, soon close enough to try to capture the castle. Weapons to fight the enemy were plentiful; cow parsley with hollow stems made strong pea shooters while willow branches made bows and arrows. No wonder no battle was ever won by the enemy.

It is said that the ghostly footsteps heard around the village of Warslow on warm summer evenings are nothing to worry about; they are just the young people of long ago enjoying themselves. But if the sound of horses hooves are heard in the distance, stand well back - it just could be a young man and his sweetheart riding off into the sunset together!

The church in the fields at Waterfall

CHAPTER 40
Winnie the flower lover at the Red Lion in Waterfall

By all accounts this is one of the best kept secrets of the Staffordshire Moorlands. A tiny village of limestone cottages and low walls hidden a little away from the main Leek to Ashborne road the A523.

This lovely village with a name which most people would think denotes a place where foaming water cascades into a dark valley floor, is said to have gained its name from the fact that the River Hamps has a delightful habit of disappearing underground near to the village. Some of the older people say with tongue in cheek that the correct name of the village should be 'Watergone'. Nevertheless the name of the village is Waterfall and what better or prettier name for such a pretty place. If any one is lucky enough to find this village, they have found a treasure.

There is no need to tell the locals who use the Red Lion public house that they are lucky - they already know. Each one of them values the peace which living in such a place brings. Not that they do not welcome those who call in as they visit the village. One of the first things a local will say to the visitor after sharing a drink with them is, " Have you seen our church?" This beautiful church was built long before either Joseph Poulton or Ralph Bullock were licensed to sell beer in the village in the early 1800s. Although mostly rebuilt at that time, some of the church dates back to Jacobean times, while parts of the chancel and a doorway have Norman origins.

One tale told to visitors perhaps to make the history of the church even more interesting, is that the reason the chancel has such a distorted shape is that many years ago a great giant tried to move the church from its place, but with its foundations buried deep into the limestone rocks, his efforts were in vain and all he managed to do was slightly dislodge it. No one knows where this legend began its life, but the oldest of the men who stand by the bar of the Red Lion know for sure that the chancel of the church was like it is long before Thomas Newton was the curate of the church in 1818.

At the same time as Reverend Newton was travelling the lanes of Waterfall telling the people in their scattered cottages of the wrath of God and how only by attending church would they be saved, the glow of Robert Wooley's fire could be seen in the village. This large man was well known for his scarred arms, each scar marking the spot were hot metal had landed causing him to jump about and spit out at great force the horseshoe nails he carried in his mouth. The colourful sparks so loved by the village children as they danced in the air, were remnants of the charges, which were used to gouge the coal from the earth, discharging in the red hot embers of the blacksmith's fire. This man mainly earned his living by replacing the metal horseshoes of the horses used to pull the heavy farm carts and farm implements. Farmhands from Master Ogden's or Master Rowe's were often to be seen leaning on the large wooden doors of the blacksmith's shop, the steam from the water-cooled metal filling, and the sound of the large hammer shaking, the air all around them, as their thoughts perhaps would wander to a pint of beer to cool the throat, in the nearby alehouse.

Not only did the blacksmith look after the farm horses, he also tended to the needs of the horses which pulled the limestone through the village on its way to be processed. These horses provided a great deal of work for him as they worked on the hard newly-laid main roads. When the railway was built, the village blacksmith was among those who objected to this form of transport and some well-educated people of the day, said. "The railway will never last and it will not take long before people realise that the best way to transport limestone is overland."

Well, as any visitor to Waterfall knows the narrow gauge railway did only last a short time. The trackway is now one of the most delightful cycle ways around, and perhaps this is one of the best ways to visit the village of Waterfall - just travelling the lanes at a pace slow enough to discover some of its well hidden secrets. Nevertheless if a cycle is the way you choose to travel, take care, besides keeping watch for passing giants, make sure you have a puncture repair kit in your bag. Because there just might be one of Mr Wooley's horseshoe nails still hidden under the grass.

CHAPTER 41
Wide-eyed Sam at the Powys Arms, Wetley Rocks

The village of Wetley Rocks is like a rough diamond, its dark rocks shining out of the greenness of the countryside. Craggy villages like Wetley Rocks are fast disappearing from the Staffordshire Moorland's landscape as people build bigger and 'better' places. But what it lacks in size, shops and discos, it makes up for in fantastic views, friendly people and solid buildings.

As well as the lovely rocks which make this village special, other landmarks make it not just a road with a rock face on one side and green fields on the other. Of all the special buildings of the village, one stands out. Although not the largest in the village, this low-roofed building is well-loved by everyone who has passed through it. The Powys Arms on the main road looks so much a part of the community that Wetley Rocks without the Powys Arms would be like a summer's evening without a pint of beer.

You can stand in the car park on any summer's day and admire a view much the same as when the Mason Arms served beer from the dark wooden bar across the road. Nothing but the memory remains of that public house now, yet perhaps the echo of the licensee calling last orders can still be heard on warm summers' evenings by those agile enough to follow the little path and climb to the summit of the rocks. Built beneath the rocks which gave the community its name and sheltered from the coldest of the north winds, the smoke from the open fires of the Mason Arms was said to be a good indication of the beer. If the grey smoke from one of the square chimney stacks was swirling round and round and blowing towards the tiny Methodist Chapel, the beer would not be as good as if the wind blew towards the wheelwright's yard!

The petrol filling station, which stands now on roughly the same spot, looks after the people of Wetley Rocks in much the same way as the public house did and like the Masons Arms, it sells so much more than the sign above the entrance suggests, even if somewhat different - a litre of five star petrol somehow does not have the same ring as a pint of black and tan.

Many of the grandsons of the farmworkers who used the Masons Arms now stand by the bar of the Powys talking late into the night about the price of cows and sheep at Leek market. These and many more are all welcomed into the long narrow rooms and with a broad smile, the question is asked many times in a day 'What's your pleasure Sir?' Yet most of the

A Pint-sized History of the Staffordshire Moorlands

Diamonds are forever at Wetley Rocks

grandfathers of today's regulars would have gone into the Powys Arms with much trepidation. Farm labourers in years gone by thought that the Powys was only for the rich people in the village, for although Wetley Rocks is mainly a farming community, there has always been wealthy people who choose to live near those lovely rocks.

The Powys Arms, or as it was once called, the Arblasters Arms, has always had connections with Lords of the Manor. The Arblasters family held the Lordship of the Manor of Cheddleton in the early 17th century and lived in nearby Rownall Hall. By the mid 18th century, the Powys family had become Lords of the Manor and moved into the Hall. To show their alliance to the Lords of the Manor and to encourage them to patronise their drinking place, they changed the name to the Powys Arms and this proved a good move as this became the place where this well-dressed follower of the King could often be found.

Many years have passed since those days, with the people who make up a full bar on a Saturday night, a mixture of all types from farmworkers who earn their living on the nearby land, to people who spend the week living and working in large cities and use the village of Wetley Rocks as a place to relax at the weekend. To the observant, although dressed differently from years gone by, they are still the same mixture of people who have always used the Powys Arms.

Yet one group of people has altered beyond all recognition over the years and that is the young people of Wetley Rocks. In times gone by a night out involved nothing more than a warm moonlit walk hand in hand along the lanes, the young man still smelling strongly of the shaving cream which was applied liberally with a stubble brush before a clean shave with a large cut-throat razor in front of tiny kitchen mirror. Holding tightly to his hand and gazing admiringly into his eyes was a young girl with just a dash of 'Evening in Paris' scent dabbed coyly behind her ears. There were no flashing games or laser shows, just the sparkle of each other's eyes and the thrill of a chaste kiss on the doorstep.

As the years pass, the sight of a young couple lost in each others arms as they plan their future together, will be as much part of the history of Wetley Rocks as the sight of a horsedrawn cart delivering beer to the Powys Arms. Perhaps in years to come even that will be forgotten. Yet a village with rocks which though dark somehow sparkle in the summer sun, can never be forgotten. Somehow they echo with all the voices of those people who have loved the area over the years.

CHAPTER 42
Blocker and his best mate at the Rose & Crown, Whitehurst

What magic ingredient changes a group of farms into a community or a community into a village? Many people will say it is the number of people working there, others will admit that no matter how many people work in an area, the magic which brings it together is first its buildings and then its people. These are the things which change a cluster of farms into a community.

Since the beginning of civilised living, the two most important buildings which brings life into an area are the place of worship and the public house. Over the years both have been the important places were people can meet and talk. Due to many factors, places of worship which once were open at all times, have now had to lock their doors when services are not taking place. That other meeting place, even though the changing attitudes to drink have brought alterations too, over the years has managed to survive as essentially the same meeting place.

Although the tiny hamlet of Whitehurst shares its important buildings with its neighbour Dilhorne, the shared landmarks have helped to give community life to Whitehurst. The tiny chapel on the corner of the lane has the title on the notice board of Dilhorne Chapel; nevertheless it is well used and well loved by members of the tiny community of Whitehurst. The wooden-floored chapel with its neatly kept garden has suffered as much as any due to the changing attitudes to religion and although services are still held inside the chapel, once the last hymn is sung and the blessing has been given, the large doors are locked until the next service.

The other landmark, the Rose and Crown public house, is a place where a thirsty man can walk in with a mind full of the worries of the world and after ten minutes, meet someone to share them with. Once inside, this public house like magic, can change an empty mug into a refreshing glass of black velvet liquid and change ordinary people into great storytellers.

The Rose and Crown, just like the chapel, is postmarked Dilhorne but it is not very often that at least two of the people at the bar ordering a pint do not call themselves Whitehurst people. This public house is not a large notable place with high-tech features and large-screen TV. It is just a cosy place with solid chairs and tables, just right for sharing an hour or two after tending the garden. Not that this pub does not welcome young people and workers; in fact around these tables can often be found the young and the not so young worker, all who use the Rose and Crown as a staging post on their way home.

To the unobservant, Whitehurst is little more than a dip in a country lane, a sharp corner, a few farms and smallholdings, one or two old cottages and in recent years a monument to the glorious dead of the war. Nevertheless there is much more than that. This is a close-knit community made up of a cross-section of people, many of whom use the tiny chapel when there is a service and the Rose and Crown in between. Like the chapel, not only is the public house the best place to visit when you are dressed up, it is just the place to visit regularly and it is the best place around to talk to people about the magic of Whitehurst.

Many hours are happily spent in the Rose and Crown re-living magical childhood memories, although the tales shared in the bar loose some of the finer facts with the passing of time. Names of those involved are forgotten and so are the exact dates but it does not matter. A tale well told, is worth its weight in gold!

The two octogenarian gentlemen who can sometimes be seen in the Rose and Crown, look just the same as other old men. With fading eyesight and hands hardly able to hold a glass steady, they both have to be helped into their seats and most of the time they can hardly remember what day of the week it is. Nevertheless, once the magic begins to work, they can talk of a time long ago, a time before the stone bridge spanned the road. Within the time it takes to order a pint of stout, the eyes of these white-haired gentlemen begin to sparkle, and a smile slowly spreads across their deeply lined faces.

It is hard at first to think of these old men as anything other than that, but after a very short time the years fall away and a picture appears of three young children no more than 8 years of age playing in the fields. Jake and Blocker along with Blocker's sister Aggie lived in one of the smallholdings along Tinkerhill Lane, not far from the high road which leads from the Kingsley Crossing to Dilhorne. Summers' days before the first war were spent playing in the fields, gathering chicken eggs from the hedgerows and taking empty bottles back for pennies. Most days would begin with the three full of energy and out exploring. As they stood on the high ground by Bank Farm with darts made out of paper, they would talk of the day that man would fly over the fields to Cheadle just like the swallows did. As the day passed the children would venture further along the lane past the small

There was a time before the stone bridge spanned the road

coal mines and on towards Dilhorne. As the shadows began to grow longer, the three would become weary of adventuring with the thought of the long walk home.

Egged on most days by Aggie, who in spite of her angelic looks was the most daring of the three, Jake, Blocker and Aggie with a basket of treasures in her hand, would first stand by the Rose and Crown waiting for a farmer and his cart to stop for refreshment. If asking, then pestering the farmer for a ride was of no avail, the three would wait for an opportune moment hid behind the low bushes opposite the Rose and Crown and then as the cart was turned and the horse set up for the journey home, the boys would jump on the back, with Aggie and her basket being hauled on without much ceremony.

Most days the three had a free ride home. One day though after collecting a rather unusually large number of eggs and a great amount of sweet blackberries, the group chose to clamber aboard a two-wheeled farm cart which stood outside the cottages next to the Rose and Crown. Settling down for a free ride home, the three made themselves comfortable in the empty cart. As the cart approached the ford in the road where the bridge now stands, without warning the carter released the handle and upturned the cart. All three landed in the cold water of the brook with eggs, blackberries and basket landing on top of Aggie. As the carter went on his way towards Whitehurst, he first turned to check all was well and then threw his head back and laughed a deep laugh which the three thought could have been heard even at the school in Dilhorne.

As the farmer and his cart disappeared along the lane to Cheadle, the boys raised their hands and promised revenge on the farmer. After retrieving caps, basket and Aggie from the water, the soggy trio walked the long way home. Feet sore from walking in wet boots, backs aching from taking turns in carrying the now crying Aggie, they were greeted by Blocker's mother who, on seeing the tear stained and wet Aggie with her dress and legs covered in a mixture of eggs and blackberry juice, thought that her delicate Aggie had been in some terrible accident.

Not waiting to wipe the baking flour from her hands or for an explanation, both boys received the devastating punishment only a mother can administer, a sharp clip with a large wooden spoon.

It was a long time before the boys were allowed out again. The rest of the summer was spent helping around the smallholding. Even when Blocker's mother could not stand the the look of torment on the boys' faces any longer, they were not allowed to take Aggie out again, for fear they might encourage her into more rough games!

As the years passed, first the boys changed to men, then the motor car replaced the farm cart, a solid bridge replaced the ford and then even, the young men, with a new found fondness for girls, changed into old men. Nevertheless, Whitehurst people only change on the outside; inside they are always the same. Even though, when they are out walking or tending the garden they need a stick to help them, once sat at the bar of the Rose and Crown, the years roll away and the real person can be seen. The community of Whitehurst will always have the magic which makes it a special place.

CHAPTER 43
Wirey Wally at the Sneyds Arms in Whiston

The community of Whiston is packed with more facts than there are drinkers in the Sneyds Arms on a Saturday night. Facts of all sorts; some like the many thousands of tons of limestone which has been transported from the nearby quarries or how the farming community has changed over the years or about the person to have a 'Hole in One' at Whiston Golf Course. But one thing that comes up in any conversation is the name of Whiston Bank, the phrase said with more reverence than if it was an international institution in London. Whiston Bank, that natural obstacle on the Staffordshire Moorland landscape has gained over the years the respect it deserves.

Although there are two completely different meanings in most dictionaries for the word 'bank', in everyday life very few people confuse the two. The first entry is the word which grew from the old Icelandic word 'Banki' which, when translated changes to the word 'Bank' as a type of elevation. This describes well that great incline leading to Whiston. The other definition has grown from the old Italian word 'Banco' or bench on which the moneychangers displayed their money many years ago. With this in mind there is never any confusion when visitors call into the Sneyds Arms and ask the way to Whiston Bank.

Many dramatic tales are told about Whiston Bank with very few of the local people going through their lives without encountering some of the difficulties this steep road holds. But there are few tales as amusing as the one told in secret about the day a set of golf clubs were bought in Whiston.

Jed was not the gentleman's real name but only with the use of a pseudonym can this story be told. As a young man he lived not far from Whiston and worked on one of the local farms. When Whiston Golf Course was first opened, young Jed's fellow workers on the farm would say mockingly "Don't expect an invite into the Golf Club house Jed, they only have well-bred folk there." Jed whose forefathers, he would tell everyone, were Lords of a Manor and only lost the Lordship through a game of poker, thought that he would show them.

With his trusty if slightly rusty bike, he set off early one morning to ask if he he could join the Whiston Golf Club. After removing his bicycle clips at the entrance and flattening his hair before putting his cap back on,

A Pint-sized History of the Staffordshire Moorlands

he made inquiries. The answer he received from a very smartly dressed man was. "Would you like to hire the Golf Clubs or did Sir have his own?" After looking at the price of hiring clubs, Jed decided that someone in the Sneyds Arms must know someone who could get him a set of golf clubs cheap.

Readjusting his cap so that the beck covered the back of his neck, back home he cycled. The following evening after work, the message was passed round the bar of the Sneyds Arms that Jed had money enough to buy a set of golf clubs. After a few days, information was received as to where a set of clubs could be brought at a reasonable price.

It's a brave man who cycles down Whiston Bank with a set of golf clubs

Well, it was hard if not impossible in places for Jed to cycle up Whiston Bank to the address he was given, but he managed. Nevertheless after a deal had been set as to what was a fair price for secondhand golf clubs. The bag with the golf clubs were securely fastened to the side of the bike and Jed thought his problems were over, well, it was all down bank now.

As he set off home with his thigh griping tightly to the bag of clubs, Jed thought he was in heaven. His thoughts were not of Whiston Bank but about long days walking around the greens and fairways of Whiston Golf Club. Then, very slowly at first, disaster began to strike.

The first thing to happen was two golf balls shot out like guided missiles from a side pocket of the golf bag. Then as the slope of the road got steeper Jed began to lose control. The bike went faster and faster. The roadside trees whizzed passed at an alarming rate and first one then another golf club jumped out of the bag. At one point Jed thought he gained control of his bike again but his heavy boots could not compete with the speed the peddles were going round.

No, the only way to end this terrifying journey was to steer off the road and into one of the banks of gravel. Even this was taken out of his hands as one of his sticking out clubs hit a tree and Jed and his bike were projected through the air. Both the bike and Jed landed in a heap in the road and for what seemed like an eternity, it rained golf clubs over Jed as he cowered under the frame of his battered bike. At last it stopped and Jed slowly sat up to survey the damage.

The road was covered with Jed's precious golf clubs and occasional golf balls still rolling and bouncing in the road like giant hailstones. Jed's bike lay in a heap with the golf bag still tied to it. Although battered and bruised, Jed was not badly hurt and still had the strength to kick the bike for its stupidity.

When he eventually arrived back at the farm, he began to sort out the damage. Despite all the trouble, only one putter was missing and two sand irons, which Jed thought he would never have need for, were bent beyond all recognition. As for the bike, which Jed was still disgusted with, that was tidied up and sold - as he said, "if it was to treat him so badly, it could not be trusted again."

Many years have passed since young Jed brought his first set of golf clubs, but whether he would ever admit now to that first purchase is debatable. Nevertheless, if at any time you are playing a round of golf at Whiston with a grey-haired man, if you know what is good for you, you won't say, "Did you buy those clubs locally?"

CHAPTER 44
Will and Walt at the Green Man, Windy Arbor

As fast cars and high speed motor bikes with loud music blaring whizz past the windows of the Green Man at Windy Arbor, young people can be heard shouting and singing on their way to the open spaces of the Peak District and Alton Towers. Locals slowly sipping their pint will often tut-tut at the sight with words such as, "I cannot understand the need people have nowadays to race everywhere. It were never like that in my day!"

Great games at Windy Arbor remembered

But the thrill of speed and the exhilaration of seeing trees fly by has always been there. Even the most sedate of these gentlemen can remember with a wry smile warm summers' evenings of long ago, a time when groups of boys in patched short trousers tied round the waist with string were a common sight racing down the road by the Green Man public house.

Youngsters of today who are too young to be in charge of petrol driven vehicles have rollerblades and skateboards to prove their prowess to one another. Wooden scooters came before these as well as carts created from orange boxes with wheels of all sizes to race against each other. Nevertheless not all games of speed were races against each other. Some games had a prize much greater than an aniseed Gob Stopper.

There was one game which is remembered with much affection by some of the old men who sit quietly now in the bar of the Green Man, which involved much more skill than deciding whether it was better to steer for the ditch and hope there was no water in it or risk scraping wooden clogs against the road. For the price of a pint and a few words of encouragement, the thrill of this speeding game is retold.

Before the game could get underway a few items were needed. Item one, and by far the most important, an empty wooden beer barrel, then a small amount of water in a jug with some one to carry it, at least two strong boys and one handkerchief preferably clean. Most of the items for the game were easy to obtain but the empty beer barrel would require a great deal of cunning. Even after all this time, information on how to obtain an empty barrel is not given freely but, by means not to be talked about, even today, the best place to lay hands on a barrel is the yard of the Green Man at Windy Arbor.

Under the cover of a stone wall and the undergrowth, water from the jug was poured carefully into the barrel and the hole plugged with the 'clean' handkerchief. The jug boy, often younger than the others, was sent with the empty jug down the road. His first job was to clear the lane of any large stones then to wait behind the wall at the end, keeping a look out for any adults (although it was never made clear what would happen if an adult was seen).

As soon as the all clear was given, with great skill the barrel was rolled down the road. As the barrel gained speed, great screams of encouragement were given by the jug boy whose head would bob up and down from behind the bushes. The barrel boys would ride, push and guide the barrel down the lane steering it the best way they could. More often than not, one of the local dogs would join in the game, barking excitedly as the group progressed down the lane.

At last, battered barrel, hot boys and yapping dog reached the bottom of the road. The now tired group of boys would just have enough strength to lift the barrel into the field. This is were the jug boy came back into his own. His job now was to carefully place the jug under the plug hole retrieve the handkerchief (which the dog would often chew for a while) and guard the barrel.

The lightly coloured liquid was then allowed to flow into the jug. How much alcohol was gathered from the sides of the barrel as the water swilled round on its journey down the hill can only be guessed at. After the jug had been passed around the group a few times, first laughter then snores could be heard from behind the hedges in the field, then all would fall silent.

As the evening light began to cast long shadows across the road in front of the Green Man, the group would be seen swaying just slightly on their way home. The jug would be returned to the kitchen table and the slightly chewed handkerchief returned to the pocket and the barrel stayed where it lay, to disappear some time later - babies always needed cots and what better shape than the rounded inside of half a beer barrel.

As the wooden barrels changed to metal kegs and the road began to get busy with cars, so the young boys with spare time and energy turned to young men tired after long days at Cauldon Lowe quarry. As with many other childhood games, this game has gradually died out. Nevertheless tucked away in the the darkest corners of the oldest barn, just maybe there is a babies cot which bears the scratches of a great race!

A FEW RECIPES GATHERED ON THE WAY

Whistler's Wonderful Damson Stout

4lbs ripe damsons.
2 pints of stout.

Method:
Half fill wide neck jars with stout.
bruise the damsons and add to the stout.
Secure the lids.
Turn every day for two weeks.
Then strain the liquid off and consume slowly.
The residue makes plant food for the garden.

Rosie's Rook Pie

6ozs flour
A little water
4oz goat's milk

Filling
pint of stock,
flour to coat
12 pigeon breasts
4 rook breasts
6oz of wild mushrooms, a little butter, a glass of oak wine or white wine.

Method:
Make pastry and chill.
Coat the breasts with flour and brown well in melted butter.
Add mushrooms and boiling stock and wine.

Put into pie dish, cover with pastry.
Decorate the top.
Cook in preheated oven 375F for 1 hour.

Bert's Best Brawn

1 pigs head & 1 pigs trotter split.
1 small onion.
Salt/pepper
1/2 oz of Gelatine.

Flavouring:
A bunch of mixed herbs.
1 dozen each allspice
         and peppercorns.
A teaspoon of grated nutmeg.
A pinch of mace.

Method:
Wash and blanch the pig's head and trotter.
Scrape and rinse well.
Put in pan with the flavouring.
Add boiling water to cover.
Cover pan and boil until the meat leaves the bones, skimming occasionally.
Remove the pig's head and trotter.
Remove tongue and skin from the pig's head.
Return all the bones to the pan and boil without the lid.
Reduce the liquor - it should be no more than a pint.
Stir in gelatine and season to taste.
While the stock is being reduced, chop meat into small pieces.
Strain reduced stock over the meat and mix well.
Transfer to a rinsed basin to set.
When firm turn out.

Alice's Apple Scones

8oz Flour.
A pinch of salt.
2 rounded teaspoonfuls
   of baking powder,
1 heaped teaspoonful
   of caster sugar,
2 oz of butter,
½ pint of milk.
2 large apples sliced
   part cooked and sweetened.

Method:
Sift dry ingredients into a bowl.
Add sugar and rub in butter.
Mix in apples and any milk which is needed to form a soft dough.
Roll out lightly on a floured board.
Cut into ½ inch thick shapes (for cooking on a griddle a little thinner)
Brush with beaten egg (for griddle cooking prick with a fork).
Bake in a hot oven for about 15 mins. (On a griddle brown lightly on both sides).
Split and spread with butter while still warm.